D1625292

NOT

MY MOTHER'S

KITCHEN

NOT

MY MOTHER'S

KITCHEN

Rediscovering Italian-American Cooking through Stories and Recipes

A Memoir With More Than 70 Recipes

ROB CHIRICO

With illustrations by the author

imagine!

A BUNKER HILL STUDIO BOOK

SOMERSET CO. LIBRARY
BRIDGEWATER, N.J. 08807

To all of the mothers who dutifully slaved over the hot stove for us, when they would rather have been doing something else. And especially to my mother, who would rather have gone bowling.

Copyright © 2016 by Rob Chirico
All rights reserved, including the right of reproduction in whole or in part in any form. Charlesbridge and colophon are registered trademarks of Charlesbridge Publishing, Inc.

An Imagine Book
Published by Charlesbridge
85 Main Street
Watertown, MA 02472
(617) 926-0329
www.charlesbridge.com

This book was designed and produced by
Bunker Hill Studio Books LLC
285 River Road, Piermont, NH 03779 • (603) 272-9221
info@bunkerhillstudiobooks.com

Library of Congress Cataloging-in-Publication Data
Names: Chirico, Rob, author.
Title: Not my mother's kitchen : rediscovering Italian-American
cooking through stories and recipes
/ Rob Chirico ; with illustrations by the author.
Description: Watertown, MA : Charlesbridge, [2016]
Identifiers: LCCN 2015037553|
ISBN 9781623545017 (reinforced for library use)
| ISBN 9781632892003 (ebook)|
ISBN 9781632892010 (ebook pdf)
Subjects: LCSH: Cooking, Italian. | LCGFT: Cookbooks.
Classification: LCC TX723 .C535 2015 | DDC 641.5945—dc23
LC record available at http://lccn.loc.gov/2015037553

Printed in the United States of America
10 9 8 7 6 5 4 3 2 1

Contents

Contents

SOUPS, SALADS, SIDES, AND SO FORTH
71

You Say Tomato, I Say Thank You! 83

Contents

PASTA

127

Contents

⌒◠

MOSTLY MEAT
169

⌒◠

Contents

PIZZA

201

LIBATIONS

211

My thought was you don't let tradition bind you. You let it set you free.

—MASSIMO BOTTURA *(Italian restaurateur and chef)*

Introduction

That's Italian! . . . Not!

My mother was an assassin.

This is a bold confession for a son to make, but it's true. My mother was an assassin—in the kitchen that is. Now please don't take this amiss. Outside of the kitchen she was one of the kindest, sweetest, and gentlest of people you could ever meet. As the writer Bill Bryson noted about his own mother, "When she dies she will go straight to heaven, but no one is going to say, 'Oh, thank goodness you're here. Can you fix us something to eat?'" I credit my love of books to my parents. Then there was music. Our home was filled with music—Broadway, jazz, Sinatra (of course), and even some opera. After all, we were Italian. But that was outside the kitchen. In front of the stove or at the microwave, my mother was the culinary equivalent of John Wilkes Booth. It has been alleged that Booth killed our country when he shot President Lincoln. My mother did the same to Italy. Martin Scorsese said, "If your mother cooks Italian food, why should you go to a restaurant?" Clearly, my mother never cooked for him.

Growing up, my conception of Italian food didn't differ much from that shared by most Americans. It was the food you were served in Italian restaurants: antipasto with olives and provolone, spaghetti and meatballs, veal Parmigiano, and lasagne with plenty of oozing mozzarella cheese. And yet, even before I ever stepped foot into a *ristorante* in Italy, the very word "restaurant" made me think of Italian food. That word evoked in me the pleasurable sensation I felt as I opened the doors and breathed in the aromas issuing from the restaurant kitchen. My sense of smell was so acute that my father once said that I had a "20-20 sniffer." Mind you, this was not a compliment, as his remark was in reference to my clipping a clothespin to my nose to block out the odor of our Friday fish cakes. At the time, though, the more pleasant aromas beckoned me to eat, not to cook.

So how does a boy go from growing up in a home where real food and a devotion to cooking were nonexistent to becoming someone who devotes considerable time every day to ruminating over the preparation and execution of every dish? I sometimes look back and wonder if my passion for good food was born out of self-defense: a defense against malformed, nearly cremated hamburgers; frozen and canned vegetables overcooked to the point that you could practically use a straw to ingest them; and, of course, so-called Italian food that was about as authentic as UFOs and Elvis sightings. But *Cacio e Pepe* (page 133) and *Raw Summer Puttanesca* (page 149) were a long way off.

Self-defense or not, even as a picky little kid—who hadn't the faintest idea that he would one day be editing cookbooks, become the winner in a national cooking competition, or spend nearly a decade working in a restaurant—I must have had an inkling that there was more to Italian cuisine than dumping Chef Boyardee Spaghetti and Meatballs into a pot. When I did begin to realize that there was more, I wanted to cook. It should have been simple. So many people did it. What I discovered over time was that there was much, much more to it than I had imagined. I'm sure I'm not alone in thinking that all I wanted to do was go into the kitchen and cook. Why did that prove so very difficult?

Back in the early 1960s, our neighborhood of Jamaica, Queens, was a mix of Italian, Polish, Irish, and Greek families. On any given summer Saturday afternoon you could hear Sinatra, polkas, the Clancy Brothers, and bouzouki music streaming from different houses. By evening time, the aromas of home cooking began to fill the air. Mrs. Giorsos baked incredible butter cookies—which made up for the stench that filled the neighborhood when she was making her own lye soap. Mr. Berezowski had a special cache of horseradish that could singe your eyebrows if you just sniffed it. I loved it, and have since grown back a full pair of eyebrows.

But the best aromas poured from the kitchens of my Italian friends. The smells of bread baking and sauce cooking permanently bathed my cousin Gerard's home. It was particularly a treat when his grandmother (my great-aunt) visited. Early in the morning she planted herself in the kitchen and spent the whole day rolling out dough and hand cutting pasta noodles. Or she would spend the day cutting up chickens for stew and chopping vegetables for her minestrone. (Had I only known at the time, I would have told her that her soup would be even better if she added a large piece of Parmigiano cheese rind.) Her spicy meatballs and tomato sauce came from recipes handed down from her mother, and, in turn, she passed the family recipes on to her daughter, my aunt Josephine. Nanny most assuredly had many of these same recipes, but my mother claimed that she never learned them because they were "Nanny's secrets."

In truth, I suspect that my mother was never interested in learning those secrets, let alone cooking the recipes. Most of my Italian friends seemed to have had families that tried to preserve at least a part of their culinary heritage, but the Italian food that we ate at home—save for the spaghetti and tomato sauce—came from the freezer or the closet: Celentano frozen *manicotti*, 4C canned Parmesan, Italian Hamburger Helper, and Noodle Roni. Occasionally there was the extra-hearty meal when she neglected to remove the plastic from the *manicotti*, which gave the cheese an entirely new dimension.

Such prepared foods were convenient for someone like my mother who clearly found cooking to be drudgery. Meanwhile, our neighborhood German delicatessen provided us with rare roast beef, potato salad, coleslaw, and other foods made daily in the back kitchen. That same deli on Parsons Boulevard—and I now apply the term "deli" loosely—has changed hands many times, and you can be sure that the roast beef today comes in a Cryovac sealed bag while the potato salad and slaw come in ten-pound buckets. With plenty of options to spare her from cooking, my mother was free to pursue activities

"Nanny" at the stove

she found much more satisfying. She sold Avon products. She liked to bowl, and her trophies proved that she was good at it. She played mahjong with her friends. She was also something of a "window lady," one of those women who enjoy spending hours sitting by the window, just watching the world go by.

On the other hand, her mother, Philomena de Marco, Nanny as I will call her, loved to cook, or so it seemed. It later became clear that it was also obligatory—her duty as woman of the house. When I was ten, I began to accompany her to the Italian shops in the Corona section of Queens. She was illiterate, and her English was still a work in progress, so I served as her interpreter. Through the heady scents that emanated from the mountains of cheeses, and the sight of the huge salamis that hung from the ceilings over the butcher counters, I was introduced to a world of cooking possibilities that lay beyond merely defrosting and baking a pan of store-bought lasagne. Those weekly trips opened my eyes to a new vista of Italian food. Still, having been fed a diet of decidedly non-Italian food, it would be a slow process before I would transcend the food I knew and reconcile myself to the food I was coming to know. The hypnotic cheeses aside, I was suspicious of anything unfamiliar. Besides, the barrels of dried *baccalà* and trays of squid were hardly tempting to me in the way that my mother's canned Franco-American Mushroom Gravy over Carl Buddig packaged turkey on Wonder Bread was. If variety is the spice of life, and Italy is no stranger to spices, I was a stranger to it all when it came to the variety of Italian cuisine.

Then there were the atrocities. One in particular was frozen spinach (which, by the way, was the first vegetable to be sold frozen, courtesy of Mr. Clarence Birdseye, who perfected frozen foods in the 1920s). The "sort of" chopped spinach my mother defrosted and cooked into a pulp made me wary of the spinach and ricotta ravioli Nanny made from scratch every Easter. Spinach was spinach as far as I was concerned, and whatever it was, I was against it. My ignorance constrained me from eating it for nearly two decades. Now, a week does not go by when I do not sauté baby spinach or any number of other simple greens with a bit of freshly chopped garlic and crushed red pepper in olive oil.

One day, as I sat on an overturned milk crate at one of the markets in Corona, I looked up briefly to watch Nanny as she griped and haggled with the store owner, Mr. Carmello. Their hands and fingers flailed about so much that you did not need to understand Italian to figure out what they were discussing. Before I could return to the affairs of Batman and Robin, his son Mimmo, who knew that this was their customary bickering, whispered to me, "Hey, kid, try this." Racked with fear of the unknown, like somebody about to bungee jump off a bridge for the first time, I held my breath as he passed me something on a wooden spoon. Now, if I was at home I would dispense with anything unfamiliar, but his broad grin alerted me that he was not out to poison me. As he brought it closer, I could see that the spoon had one small piece of their sausage on it. The sausage was covered with a thick mahogany sauce the likes of which I had never seen. At that point, however, I hesitated only briefly because the sausage, with a light dusting of grated cheese, was as alluring to the eye as it was to my nostrils. I thought I could almost see a tangible wisp of the aroma rise upward from the small spoon. It was almost like a wispy finger in an old Daffy Duck cartoon, beckoning me.

Ah, but when I tried it, it was the meaty sauce that was unlike anything I had ever tasted. Somehow the tomatoes were different. They seemed to have a salty sweetness all their own, without a hint of bitterness or artificial sweetness. Despite how much this sauce opened my eyes as well as my nostrils, I much prefer removing the sausage from its casings when I make my *Pappardelle with Spicy Sausage Sauce* (page 144) for a more meaty, concentrated flavor.

I imagine that Nanny could have made such a tantalizing sauce, and she probably did—but, compliant as she was to my grandfather while he was alive, she did not make red sauce very often. In part this may have been because my fully Americanized grandfather did not care much for pasta. I should mention here that theirs was a prearranged marriage. As was the case with the other five million, mostly southern, Italians who arrived on Ellis Island at the turn of the last century, she was hoping for a better life here. To escape *la miseria*—the poor conditions of so much of southern Italy—she was willing to face the unknown, and a language she did not understand, to wed a man she had never met.

On this side of the globe, my grandfather was born in New York City and considered himself more American than Italian. He even abandoned his given name Pasquale for the Irish-sounding Pat. With the Irishman "Big Tim" Sullivan leading Tammany Hall, which had provided work for ethnic groups when few others did, this was probably a good idea. As a construction worker on the Sixth Avenue El train, my grandfather much preferred the mammoth portions of steaks and potatoes that were served in the States to a humble plate of "spaghett." With the stories of his parents' homeland still in his blood, though, his Italian side would oftentimes break through at the sight of such American staples as oatmeal. He laughed and called it animal food, because that's what he was told his father had fed horses in Italy. When I recall Grandpa's stony-faced visage, I can still see him hunched over in the single chair he always sat in, reading the *Daily News* and puffing on his prized El Producto Queen cigars. He spoke little, and of that modicum of speech, none was reserved for complimenting my grandmother's cooking, least of all her pasta sauce.

As a brief family aside, I really don't know much about my father's parents. They also came over in the great Italian wave of immigrants at the turn of the previous century. Two children were in tow, but my father, who was the youngest, was born here. His mother died two months before I was born, and his father lived in Brooklyn with the rest of the Chirico family. Oddly, they Americanized the name and spelled it "Cherico," which almost sounds Native American. I saw little of my grandfather. This was because we had no car, and the time it took to travel to Brooklyn by train was tantamount to crossing half of the United States by covered wagon. Perhaps it was not to hurt my mother by insulting her cooking (my sister and I were there for that), but my father rarely spoke of the food he grew up with. I knew more about what he ate in the Air Force—some meat extrapolation with gravy that he referred to as "S on a shingle." My father never swore. He left that to Nanny and Grandpa.

Thinking back to Mr. Carmello's red sauce, I may have relegated it to my visual and olfactory memory, because at one Sunday meal I was nearly floored by my mother's spaghetti sauce. It was decidedly different. First of all, the color was more of a bright crimson than the usual bland puddle of dull red. And, like the sauce I had tasted from Mimmo's spoon, it possessed a sweetness not born from sugar, but from the tomatoes themselves. No, it wasn't as rich as the sauce I had tasted in Corona, but it was also not as bland as my mother's usual sauce. After several twirls and forkfuls of spaghetti, I finally asked my mother what brand of tomatoes she had used for the sauce. Accustomed to the family's often unwarranted complaints, she defensively pointed her fork at me and asked, "Why? What's wrong with it?" I said, "Nothing," because the sauce was really good. And I meant *really* good. I told her that she should keep buying those tomatoes. I read the label on the can, Luigi Vitelli. These were actually whole tomatoes, instead of the purée she usually bought. I much later learned that Luigi Vitelli imported Italy's finest tomatoes from San Marzano sul Sarno in Campania. With no inducement besides "really good," she resumed her requisite Sunday sauce-making with whatever canned puréed tomatoes that were on sale.

I think it's pretty clear by now that enjoying Italian food at home was a rarity, as was hearing the Italian language. The main reason there was no Italian spoken was not because we were to be fully Americanized, as was the case in my father's household growing up. My parents could not speak Italian. Just like the American English that we exclusively spoke, our meals were comparably limited in their ethnicity. Despite having no guidance in the preparation of Italian food, I somehow imagined that I knew all about Italian cooking, as if it were vicariously assimilated just by being Italian (and, as I wish the Italian language could be). This, of course, was an enormous blunder. My first attempts at making red sauce during my college years should be allocated to the Museum of Major Mistakes. Even I could see that the pathetic pot of viscous, bitter sauce could only be masked by mountains of grated cheese.

As I became more interested in knowing about food and cooking, I also discovered that there was more than just bad cooking; there was bad food—the sell-by-whenever packages that could sit in a supermarket shelf for weeks without witnessing the slightest metamorphosis. When I visited Italy for the first time in the late 1970s on a travel grant, I did not see this "miracle" of preservation. A shop that was filled with foodstuffs early in the day was almost empty by nightfall. The concept of shelf life had seemingly not reached their shores—yet. As I became more familiar with fresh foods and ingredients back home, I became equally aware that unlike the fresh food of my Italian ancestors, ours was overprocessed and filled with additives.

It was in graduate school in the '70s, when I was given that travel grant to prepare for my PhD orals exam, that I experienced the Mediterranean diet and saw firsthand how Italians cooked and ate. Being in Italy afforded me the opportunity to experience the cooking of my ancestors. It inspired me to try to create the dishes I had never had at home. I also learned that you need not spend an eternity whipping up a fine meal. A simple plate of pasta with garlic, oil, and hot pepper can be as satisfying as a sauce that has simmered for hours. Still, although I was awakened to the food of Italy and the Italian way of eating, I also came to more fully appreciate the fine foods and cooking my homeland had to offer.

While I strive to re-create many authentic Italian dishes at home today, much of my own cooking may seem quite individual next to traditional Italian fare—but so is Italian cooking from one region to the next. Most of the recipes I reproduce in this volume are variations on an Italian theme rather than a direct transcription. I like to think that my Bucatini all'Amatriciana or Balsamic Roasted Chicken are not far cries from the dishes I tasted in Rome and Modena, but I know that my version of a meat ragù in the style of a Bolognese (made with savory lamb and peppery rosemary instead of beef) might raise some eyebrows—if not a meat cleaver over my head. While some of the recipes here are my takes on the familiar, they are mostly the result of the years I have spent "dancing" with them in the kitchen. It may seem like a ridiculously moot point, but I personally prefer to think of this style of cooking as "American Italian." While it may be rooted in Italian cooking, it is more often my American variation of it. And let us bear in mind that pizza is one of the world's favorite dishes due to its having been made so popular here. With the influx of Neapolitan immigrants to the East Coast, their regional dish of pizza was more familiar to the Italians in cities like New York and New Haven than it was in Italy. It wasn't until the 1950s that pizza began to catch on in the "Old Country." Today, Italians consume a total of about 2.5 billion pizzas a year—thanks to their Neapolitan emigrants.

I see the blending of American and Italian foods and methods as a *matrimonio felice*—a happy marriage—just as each person in a partnership carries into it something unique to themselves and retains something unique unto themselves, and joined together they create a blissful union. I applaud tradition, but I continually experiment—just as my ancestors undoubtedly did. I also like to believe that my experimentation has taught me to be true to the ingredients at hand. I have seen restaurant and cookbook concoctions perpetrated under the name of experimentalism or, worse, creativity. As one venerable Italian told me, "Cook with your heart and stomach, not with your eyes and head."

You may study and come close to re-creating a few of the "classic" dishes of a particular country, but it is far more important to appreciate the different flavors and ideas in the hope of expanding your own culinary horizons. As a cook of Italian descent, I hope to sensibly embrace that happy marriage between the foods and cooking from here and abroad. To hack a quote from *Candide's* Dr. Pangloss, present-day Italian American cooking may just be "the best in this best of all possible worlds."

Every Cook and Nanny, or Pass the Porkette, Please

The only cookbook I remember seeing at home when I was growing up was Peg Bracken's witty *I Hate to Cook Book*, which my mother probably never read. If she ever did attempt to embark upon the recipe for a quick stroganoff, I can see her as a striking example of Ms. Bracken's advice: "Start cooking those noodles, first by dropping a bouillon cube into the noodle water. Brown the garlic, onion, and crumbled beef in the oil. Add the flour, salt, paprika and mushrooms, stir, and let cook five minutes while you light up a cigarette and stare sullenly at the sink."

This is not to say that my mother did not try to cook in our rabbit warren. How could one be an assassin, even a kindly one, without a weapon? In my mother's hands, every kitchen appliance or utensil was hers. Left to her own devices she laid waste to spaghetti, hamburgers, and even salad. "Fresh" was not a word she used, unless it was leveled at me— and deservedly so. I confess that, as young kids are wont to do, I routinely rudely complained about my food. As a child I may have known nothing about lamb, but I did not think that it should be the same texture as my canvas Chukka boots. Perhaps I have Bugs Bunny to thank for my enjoyment of raw carrots, but the little orange cubes that nestled together in a tin can with tiny, squishy, pallid pellets that passed themselves off as peas were a species in their own right. If it had not been for the fresh peas that Nanny once prepared, I might have concluded that most vegetables were of dubious merit at best.

Please pass the lasagne, sweetie.

Nevertheless, I don't know if Nanny was out to preserve traditions and pass them on to anyone. This grey-haired, seemingly perennially aproned woman basically cooked the American meals that her husband and son expected. Save for holidays, when she cooked Italian, it was usually in small amounts just for herself. I have begun to wonder in retrospect if she did really enjoy cooking, or if it was just a requirement: the need to cook for and feed others. She once said, "If anything happens to me, what will happen to the squirrels?" I thought that this was a translation of one of those venerable Italian sayings that we do not understand until we are much older—and, hopefully, wiser. I still am unclear and hope that this is a sign for the need for longevity.

Furthermore, as to cooking in the Italian style back then, apart from making long trips to markets in Corona, the Bronx, or Little Italy, you simply could not find good Italian ingredients in our local stores. By 1960, even shops that began to stock Italian ingredients sorely lacked essential or merely common Italian staples: fresh basil, pine nuts, squash blossoms, cardoons, Parmigiano-Reggiano, extra-virgin olive oil (even the name "extra-virgin" would have produced sly giggles), and *pancetta*—let alone *guanciale* or *lardo*. This has all changed, thankfully, but even if you had heard of a curiosity such as *pesto* back then, our nearby King Kullen supermarket most assuredly did not have the makings for it.

Judging from what he ordered in restaurants, my father's palate was much more expansive than my mother's. It was only much later that I figured out that he was forced to forgo many of the dishes that he had grown up with. As a pre-teen, there was nothing to prepare me for *trippa*, which he ordered one time in an Italian restaurant in Little Italy. He gave me a taste, and my jaded palate only registered that interlaced web of cow's stomach lining as a bicycle inner tube exploding with broken watch springs. I would have preferred cat food. He praised the restaurant's escarole soup, but my mother could not, or would not, make that either. As it was for so many men of his generation, his sole cooking domain before he retired was the barbecue grill. I still recall the crisp snap of hot dogs and the great juicy steaks, all the while assuming that grilled food was supposed to taste like Kingsford lump charcoal doused with quarts of lighter fluid. It all tasted good back then. Of course, I now know that those chemicals are odious. Still, the burgers and dogs certainly "hit the spot" at the time, and it is with great fondness that I look back at the Fourth of July parties in our small backyard.

Then there was the way we ate. It was fine for us, but it was also not Italian. Our meals were served up just the way most Americans still eat at home: "family style." Unlike Italians in Italy, who ate a succession of courses, our

Mom and Dad in their home in Queens

dinner was basically a one-course meal. It may have consisted of several dishes, such as meat, potatoes, and a vegetable, but everything came out at once. If the dinner was spaghetti and meatballs, and maybe a salad, it all appeared and was eaten at the same time. There was also a plate of white bread and a side of butter. This was not in keeping with the history of the world and the devotion to the staff of life that serves us all; the Wonder Bread was there just in case we did not eat the rest of the meal. I loved its soft, pillowy texture, only much later to conjecture that this was because it was used to stuff pillows. That cold pat of butter, which tore into the bread, was there as a supplement to fill our bellies if we did not finish our canned peas and carrots and our pork tenderloin. This I later learned was not tenderloin at all, but a fatty, unctuous boiled Freirich *Flavor* Porkette, aka pork shoulder butt. At the time I knew better, or so I thought. The meat was neither tender nor a loin. I even wondered whether it was a shoulder or a butt, but what did I truly know?

Least of all, did I know that we were stretching the paycheck until it bled? I'm not mentioning this to make you feel sorry for us (though sympathy is always welcome), but to point out that given that I was used to eating foods that were akin to plaster of Paris, I was totally unaware of the wide array of marvelous foods that were available—foods that were both healthful and edible. As I did begin to learn, I naturally began to spend more on finer ingredients. My father was later wont to say regarding this growing partiality, "Champagne taste on a beer salary." He had something there, since he could never imagine spending twice the amount of money on a box of imported De Cecco pasta over Ronzoni. I am certain, though, that my father had never read A. J. Liebling, who partially vindicated this penchant in *Between Meals* when he wrote, "A man who is rich in his adolescence is almost doomed to be a dilettante at the table. This is not because all million-aires are stupid but because they are not impelled to experiment."

Holidays were different. This was when uncles, aunts, and their entourage all arrived, and Nanny went all out. As befitting an Italian American house-hold, we had to indulge in a requisite fifteen-pound trencher of lasagne before the other hundred or so dishes of glazed ham, roast turkey, fluffy mashed potatoes, sweet potatoes (sans marshmallows), crisp green beans, and salad came out practically at the same time. There is the old joke that goes like this: "The trouble with eating Italian food is that five or six days later you're hungry again." If the way Italians ate was a delicate sonata with several movements, a typical American meal was something of a loaded jam session. I also want to stress here that on a typical day, dinner was our main meal, whereas in Italy, lunch was and still is. Of all the statistics available on Italy and its varied economic prob-lems, few are as eye-opening as the fact that at around one p.m. on any given day, more than half

A happy holiday conversation…

the population will normally be sitting down to a long and leisurely lunch. Our American lifestyle and working habits have sadly, but often necessarily, prohibited this slower paced tradition.

Slow Learner

During my graduate school year, I met my wife-to-be, Valdina. When we moved in together in her grandmother's minuscule apartment on the Upper East Side, Soup Burg takeout bags were replaced with Gristede's grocery bags. Cooking was becoming an avocation—a happy pastime. That cook-ing would evolve into a devotion was something I could not have dreamed of even on opium. My true early days as an aspiring young cook would not take place in that tiny apartment, though, but in Valdina's family manse, a three-story house overlooking Long Island Sound in Stamford, Connecticut. Moreover, it was more of an accident that I only half jokingly attribute to boredom—an escape from suburban cocktail-hour conversation.

As art dealers, Valdina's parents were continually throwing parties for friends and prospective clients. Not caring to socialize with most of the guests, I offered my services to Valdina's mother in the kitchen. Gradually I took over the reins, and we were both happy to forgo our unenviable positions. At the time it was just a means of escape, but it did mean I had to cook—and however pedestrian it might have been at first, cook I did.

One thing about escape is that you also find others who wish to be in the same boat, away from the sinking ship of tired conversation. Usually the folks who were also bored with the party sought solace in the kitchen. Not surprisingly, they were also probably the most interesting of guests, and I had many fine chats with fellow fugitives. During my time alone, I discovered that the kitchen had a small selection of cookbooks, thanks to a subscription to Book-of-the-Month Club. Among them were *The Joy of Cooking* (of course), James Beard's *American Cookery*, Julia Child's *Mastering the Art of French Cooking*, and, perhaps most important of all for me, Marcella Hazan's *The Classic Italian Cookbook*. It did not seem all that long before I graduated from being party chef and became would-be home cook. I was soon making our meals every night: lasagne with Bolognese and béchamel sauces, roast chicken with rosemary, and *pesto*. (I finally understood what could be done with the bushels of basil that my mother grew!)

After such a slow start, what followed seemed to happen so quickly. It was as if I had been doing this all my life, even with the dismal failures I have needed therapy to forget. After our move to Connecticut in the early '80s, I was suddenly no longer receiving turtleneck sweaters and sweat suits from my wife for my birthday, but Sabatier carbon-steel knives. Her biggest coup may have been the five-piece hand hammered French copper cookware that was on closeout at Bloomingdale's for $350.

It was particularly fortuitous that with much of Stamford still having a large Italian community, there was a fabulous supermarket appropriately called Bongiorno's. Its shelves were overstocked with every manner of produce and Italian food products that were almost impossible to find outside of New York City. Naturally, it helped that I was teaching at the Fashion Institute of Technology in Midtown Manhattan, and whatever I could not find locally was available to me in Little Italy. In retrospect I can see that I was just a novice, but I was a dedicated one. I still had many years of practice and experimentation ahead of me. Mistakes were bound to happen, and they certainly did. But it is no secret that we can learn from them and, hopefully, not repeat them. (Try adding lemon pepper to an onion soup. *No, don't!* A jar of lemon pepper has a place, but not in the kitchen.)

Again, it was thanks to my graduate school travel grant that I discovered how and what Italians in Italy ate. I learned that a small portion of pasta or a moderate bowl of soup was always a first course. In fact, even the starter course in Italy is called *minestre*, which literally translates as "soup" (but more on that later). A plate of piquant *Spaghetti con Aglio e Olio* (Spaghetti with Garlic and Olive Oil), also being a first course, was served in the same type of soup plate. Accordingly, this was followed by a second dish of, say, *Scaloppine di Vitello alla Pizzaiola* (Veal Scaloppine with Tomatoes), accompanied by sautéed spinach, after which might come a salad, and then fruit and cheese. This tradition dates back to ancient Rome. The Romans' expression for it was *"ab ovo ad mala"* (from eggs to apples). A customary meal in an Italian *ristorante* was a progression of complimentary and complementary tastes that all blended in harmony and pleased all of the senses.

For me, however, growing up eating mediocre fare, and then discovering that food should be anything but, it started me on a lifelong journey of how to cook. Still, this journey has been a long work in progress: a quest, if you will. And like any dutiful quest, when properly begun, it has no end. Is that a bit quixotic? You bet. Lastly, to quote the singular and feisty Jim Harrison from *The Raw and the Cooked*, "If I don't enjoy myself in this life, when am I going to enjoy myself?"

A Note on the Recipes
(or "Broiler Alert")

∽

The definitive recipe for any Italian dish has not
yet appeared. We are still creating.
—LUIGI BARZINI

Recipes in cookbooks are generally curious phe-
nomena. They seem to have arrived fully formed, like Venus rising from
the sea, without a hint of the time and effort that preceded them. With this
book being a reminiscence as well as a cookbook, what I want to show is
how I arrived at developing these recipes that have become a part of my life.
From the beginning I had no intention of creating yet another Italian book
of recipes. I wanted to share the dishes my present family loves with the
stories of how the dishes came about over the years. For example, how do
you make meat *ragù* after seeing a dozen or more ways to prepare it, or how
do you replicate a dish that you have heard of, like a mortadella sauce, but
have not seen a serviceable recipe for?

Along with the anecdotes and reflections, I have also incorporated historical tidbits: Did you know that the original version of *Caesar Salad* did not
contain lemon or anchovies? Some additional trivia: Italians consider it bad
luck to cut rather than tear basil. Facts: as much as 50 percent of the olive
oil sold in America is, to some degree, fraudulent. And tips that I learned
through trial and (much) error: Salt can kill yeast. Do not add it to your
pizza dough until it has begun to come together. Also, heating lemons or
oranges in a microwave for about 10 seconds will yield more juice. There

is also the occasional quote: "There's nothing more romantic than Italian food" (Elisha Cuthbert). Agree or disagree with the romantic part, but . . . on second thought, don't disagree.

I have not included anything that I do not cook—or at least have not cooked. There is no filler here, except perhaps in the *Stuffed and Rolled Peppers, Lipari Style* (page 118). I do not own a cookbook from which I have tried every recipe, and I do not want to bog you down with recipes you may already know or ones so complicated or esoteric that you would have an easier time reading a stereo manual. (True, Francis Mallmann's recipe in *Seven Fires* for cooking an entire 1,400-pound cow is a fun read, but who has heavy-duty block and tackle attached to a steel stanchion set in concrete, along with two cords of hardwood logs, perched behind the Weber kettle and the 10-pound bag of hardwood charcoal? (I go through four cords of firewood during the course of an entire Massachusetts winter.)

Naturally, many of the recipes herein are adaptable as well. I include only one *risotto* and one egg *frittata* recipe, but they can serve as springboards for your own creativity. In the end, this is a reflection on growing up in an Italian American family that recognized its roots, but hardly its culinary inheritance—the latter of which I hope to have rectified here.

One very important lesson I have learned when embarking on a new recipe is that you should never prepare it for anyone but family or close friends your first time trying it—and even the latter may be inviting trouble. This is not merely to avoid embarrassment if something goes amiss, but also because you simply might not be interested in having it again. Apart from desserts, most recipes are malleable. After making one for the first time, you may want to tweak it to suit your own taste.

Recipes are guides that take you on a specific path, but that does not mean that you cannot take minor steps to smell the basil along the way. Remember also that, apart from baking, recipes are not "paint by numbers." You should always feel free to alter a dish to suit your own taste (as you no doubt already do with the recipes you love). I personally approach some recipes as I would a mystery novel, trying to follow the leads until the investigation is complete. Unlike with a novel, however, I have no difficulty in altering the aspects of the plot that I think could work better another way. In that respect, this book is my mystery novel. As much as I trust in the outcome, you should feel no qualms about occasionally thickening the plot—or the sauce—when you deem it necessary.

Among the few less salty phrases heard in a restaurant kitchen is "Get your *mise* in order." This is short for *mise en place*, or setting up all you need before you start cooking. It's maddening to realize that you can't find the parsley when you start cooking—or worse, that you find that you have none. If you set everything out ahead of time, cooking will proceed smoothly and quickly. And clean as you go. CAYG! You want to enjoy your meal, and after you're done, you want to relax. Going into a kitchen with the sink lined with pots and pans is just miserable. Once you get into the habit of rinsing out those ramekins or bowls for garlic and onions just after you've finished with them, those are two fewer things to deal with later. Anything you can clean or stick in the dishwasher before you sit down to eat will only make the cleanup easier and faster.

Ingredients

*Don't eat anything your great-grandmother
wouldn't recognize as food.*

—MICHAEL POLLAN

Aside from the tomatoes Nanny grew in summer, those that insulted our table the rest of the year were the uniform orange spheroids that came in a cellophane-wrapped package—as did our puny little heads of garlic. Pre-packaging was the way to go for modern America—and the way it almost always went in our home. About the only vegetables (apart from the orange spheroids) that were common to our household were iceberg lettuce and fennel, the latter of which my father had a penchant for. He loved his salads. Since cheese was already grated and arrived in a cylindrical container, I had no inkling that you should buy your own and grate it yourself. For the most part, my brief comments about foodstuffs will partly be about what it was like growing up on a desert island mostly devoid of quality ingredients.

My father and his beloved salad

On a brief but more serious note, with the ever-increasing domination of the commercial food industry over local purveyors, the consumer must become more and more of a supermarket sleuth. Ask questions and read labels, because you may not be getting what you think. The federal government is not helping us on this. In March of 2013, the Monsanto Protection Act was signed into law, by President Obama, no less. This effectively bars federal courts from being able to halt the sale or planting of GMO crops and seeds, no matter what health consequences from the consumption of these products may come to light in the future. Even if crops are found to be dangerous or to cause a runaway crop plague, the U.S. government now has no judicial power to stop them from being planted or harvested. It lost its funding due to public outcry, but there are attempts to revitalize it. Before you buy those ears of genetically modified corn, be aware that not only are they severely lacking in vitamins and nutrition compared to non-GMO corn; they also pose numerous health risks due to pesticides and toxic chemicals found in GMO corn. Would you care for a dollop of something like "Golly, Gee! I Know Darned Well This Isn't Butter!" with that? So is the question we should ask, "Who's running whom?" Or is it "Who's killing whom?"

Cheese

The French claim that they have one cheese for every day of the year, although they do not specify which cheese for each day. Italians are no less generous in their cheese production. This being the case, save for some of the nearly omnipresent mozzarella and hard grating cheeses discussed here, I will address specific cheeses such as Gorgonzola and provolone in their respective recipes.

The cheese most commonly found in our fridge when I was growing up was either a slab of Velveeta or a jar of Cheez Whiz. When my father began collecting Social Security, he was eligible to bring home "government cheese" (pronounced *guv-mint*). This was a solid block of unspecified yellow dairy matter that was purported by the government to "slice and melt well." Nothing was said about taste or nutritional value. Naturally we had "Parmesan" cheese in our household—if you can count the ground-up likes of a cue ball in a cardboard shaker as cheese. I do recall that we had a four-sided cheese grater. This was exclusively reserved for mozzarella, since no one had come up with the dubious idea for packaged shredded mozzarella yet. What the other three sides of the grater were for remained an enigma. Things have not changed much for my mom. The last time I made dinner for her, I brought a chunk of Parmigiano-Reggiano (never having acquired a taste for cue ball). No grater was to be found. I believe that Microplanes are the best for harder cheese, and what started out as a carpenter's tool now comes in a multitude of shapes and grating sizes. The old-fashioned box style that has two sandpaper-like sides is mostly worthless. It is indeed the lesser of two graters.

Most of the mozzarella that one finds in stores is fairly lifeless. The best that can be said about the majority of commercial brands is that the cheese melts well (like government cheese?). Artisanal cheesemakers are now producing excellent fresh mozzarella from cow's milk. In the opinion of many, the finest cheeses, *mozzarella di bufala*, are still produced in southern Italy from a special breed of water buffalo. The Nazis killed off most of the herds during the retreat from Italy in World War II, but the herds have since been restocked from animals imported from India. Buffalo mozzarella is again common, although the buffalo milk is often blended with a large percentage of cow's milk. So far the attempts to raise this curious breed of animal in the United States have yet to yield a comparable cheese. Italian buffalo mozzarella, packed in water, is rather expensive because it has a shelf life of only a few days, and must therefore be flown in from Italy daily.

If you are only able to procure commercial mozzarella, shred it and blend it with a good olive oil to enhance the flavor. I have found that Polly-O and Trader Joe's have fared best among packaged block (not pre-shredded) cheeses for melting. I emphasize "for melting" because they are otherwise still rather bland if eaten raw. I would also still encourage adding olive oil to your freshly grated cheese and letting it sit for about an hour before you plan on using it. Lastly, since whole milk mozzarella really only has a gram or two of extra fat per serving versus part-skim mozzarella, why bother with the latter? Also you could try making your own mozzarella. It's actually fairly simple to prepare from scratch, but even simpler if you can buy fresh cheese curds. The process can take less than 30 minutes using the latter, and not much more with the former. Videos for making your own mozzarella abound online.

True Parmigiano-Reggiano is unique in that its distinctive flavor is due to the specific environment in which the cows graze: a small area in the Emilia-Romagna region of northern Italy. The fermentation process, which lasts eighteen months, has gone on unchanged for over seven hundred years, producing one of the finest cheeses on earth. With that kind of history, why would anyone want to waste money by buying a gritty, grated sack of fluff? Whereas almost all Parms are created equal, they frequently don't end up that way. A buttery, amber chunk cut fresh from the wheel bears no comparison to the chalky, dehydrated lump that has languished for days on end in the supermarket cheese bin.

If I say that "almost" all true Parms are created equal, there are at least two exceptions. One is a Parmigiano made by a farmhouse dairy in the remote mountains outside of Modena: *Vacche Rosse*, or Red Cow Parmigiano. Using only the raw, untreated rich cow's milk from the original, now rare, Red Cow breed of cattle, only a few farmers have taken the care and attention needed to raise these special cows. The aging process can take up to twice as long as with regular Parm. As you might expect, the price is consequently at least twice that of regular Parmigiano—if you can even find it (see the Mail-Order Sources).

Then there is the Parmigiano-Reggiano *Stravecchio*, which is aged a full thirty-six months. At this age, it has a deeper golden color and has even more crunchy crystals. Full and fruity with a slightly salty tang, this cheese should be served in chunks with fine balsamic vinegar, figs, or pears as an appetizer with an aperitif or after a meal. To keep the cheese as fresh as possible, never grate it until you are ready to use it; and store it in wax paper wrapped with foil, since plastic film will suffocate the cheese over long periods of time. And never throw away the rind! It is a marvelous addition to soups and stocks.

Grana is the catchall term for any hard grating cheese, but Grana Padano, like Parmigiano-Reggiano, is governed by strict regulations and must pass quality tests before its rind is fire-branded with the Grana Padano trademark. The younger Grana Padano is aged for only a year and is less crumbly, milder, and not as complex in flavor as Parmigiano-Reggiano, or even its own Grana Padano Riserva, which is aged for twenty months. Seeing that *Grana Padano* is Italy's most popular (and most consumed) hard cheese, it is certainly a satisfactory substitute for Parm when the coffers are running low or when you need copious amounts for a recipe. At the other end of the taste spectrum of popular grating cheeses, Pecorino Romano (from the Italian *pecora* for "sheep") is a saltier, more piquant cheese made from ewe's milk. Romano should be used for its own unique flavor or in dishes where Parmigiano-Reggiano would otherwise be overwhelmed.

One other use of cheese in Italy unknown to Americans is its place in name-calling. If you happen to play a particularly bad hand in cards, you may just get the word *provola* hurled at you. Being classified as a mozzarella is not very different from being termed more generically a cheesehead.

Cured Meats

As far as good cured meats go, our house decidedly went in the opposite direction. This could be said of the nation at large. The extent of our knowledge of *salumi* was salami and pepperoni, the latter not even being an Italian immigrant but an American-born article. Moreover, the term "pepperoni" is not even properly Italian, as it is a corruption of *peperoni*, the plural of *peperone*, the Italian word for "bell pepper." The true Italian *salumi* repertoire includes such meats as *guanciale*, *coppa* (or *capicola*), *spalla*, *'nduja*, *lardo*, *lonza*, *pancetta*, prosciutto, and, of course, salami, but in the 1960s you were at a loss to find any but the last two. And even they were exclusively made in

Pancetta

the United States. It was not until 1990 that Italian prosciutto was allowed into the country. When Ada Boni's important *Italian Regional Cooking* appeared on our shores in 1969, it boasted more than six hundred "authentic" recipes. True, there is a dish titled in Italian *Spaghetti al Guanciale*, but its translation beneath is "Spaghetti with Bacon." The recipe itself does not call for *guanciale* or even *pancetta* but—you guessed it—bacon. Regarding *pancetta*, it is customarily found sliced or in chunks in supermarkets. If you can get hold of slab *pancetta*, which is usually artisanal, I not only find it more flavorful, it is much easier to work with. Older cookbooks will tell you what to substitute for *pancetta*: There is no substitute.

Thanks to the Internet, we live in a time when we can finally begin to cook Italian food the way it was meant to be. Recently the USDA lifted the long-standing ban on the importation of many more Italian cured meats, as long as the producers follow (the often archaic) USDA regulations and bear the expense of full-time, on-site USDA inspectors. There is some irony in this. Cured meats such as prosciutto are forbidden by Italian law to include sugar, water, nitrites, or any additives except a minimum of salt (all of which are quite common in many American products). In fact, the word "salami" is derived from the Latin *sal* (salt), which was the earliest preservative used in curing sausages. Do you crave coppa made from Cinta Senese pigs? It is just a click away. In the meantime, La Quercia of Norwalk, Iowa, makes an outstanding array of cured and specialty meats.

A curious war made San Francisco the salami capital of America. From 1967 until 1970, a band of six determined Bay Area sausage makers argued to the U.S. Department of Agriculture that they deserved the right not only to use Italian methods, but to call their product "Italian salami." They were direct descendants of salami makers of Milan, Lucca, Parma, and Modena. Around the turn of the last century, they had settled in a city whose temperate climate might be the only one in the United States perfectly suited for dry-curing salami. They even had the right strain of penicillin mold to give the links a classic white bloom. I would highly recommend any of San Francisco's Molinari cured meats. Their salami, Finocchiona salami, Toscano salami, hot salami, and *coppa* have been slaking cravings for over a hundred years.

Garlic

That versatile, indispensable knobby cluster of happiness was almost entirely ornamental for my family, and it was not a pretty sight at that. Our heads of garlic did not have teeth; they had dentures. Rather than succumb to the mythic prowess of garlic, vampires would have died laughing if confronted by our miserable specimens. The only garlic I remember seeing in our home came two to a package. The measly heads would sit there beneath their plastic wrapper shield until they shriveled into oblivion, leaving their dusty empty skins for one to ponder what the purpose of their contents had been in the first place.

The word "garlic" comes from the Old English *garleac,* meaning "spear leek." Dating back over six thousand years, the plant is native to Central Asia. Over the centuries garlic was mostly demeaned as unpleasant peasant food: It "maketh a man wynke, drynke, and stynke." American journalist and humorist Arthur Baer warned, "There is no such thing as a little garlic." Contrary to the stereotype, however, Italians are not great consumers of the "stinking rose." One finds it mostly in southern Italian cooking and almost not at all in traditional northern Italian cooking, although it's hard to imagine a classic dish like *ossobuco alla Milanese* without a hint of garlic. Continuing down the leg of the boot, we can see that Roman cooking is something of a middle ground. Classics such as the *Amatriciana* (actually from the Abruzzo region but made famous in Rome) and *Cacio e Pepe* sauces are garlic-free, but garlic is the soul of *Spaghetti con Aglio, Olio, e Peperoncino.* Our association of Italy with garlic is probably due to the southern Italians who immigrated to different countries and brought their use of garlic with them. While garlic has unshackled itself from the onus of peasant food in the north, it is yet an unreservedly welcome guest.

Moreover, some Italian critics adamantly complain that the bulbous herb reeks and overwhelms more delicate flavors. Filippo La Mantia, a chef who worked at La Trattoria in Rome, shunned garlic saying that it was a leftover from when Italians were poor and used it to flavor their meager victuals. To the contrary, garlic aficionados say that in the right amount, it enhances and embellishes otherwise bland dishes. While that could be said of almost anything, the thousands of people who flock to garlic festivals across the country would agree when it comes to that pungent little bulb. Proponents now advocate for garlic's influence in strengthening our immune system, among other health benefits.

Garlic abounds in summer. I may have eight varieties to work with from local farmers, but for our purpose here, I would recommend the larger, readily available, compact purple-skinned bulbs that have a pungent yet sweet flavor. Young garlic still has its scallion-like green stem that may be cooked like a scallion. As the season goes on, garlic is only thinking of itself. It will naturally want to flower, and it begins to grow from within. At this point the clove, or "tooth," will begin to develop a greenish "stinger" that can be bitter. I suggest that you slice the clove in half lengthwise and cut out the little bugger.

In any season, whether it is simmered in braises or sautéed in oil, garlic has a limitless role in cooking. Since garlic cloves vary dramatically in size, I could never accept why almost all recipes specify garlic by the number of cloves alone. Certainly you can use your judgment, but for the sake of consistency I have given a specific measurement as a guide. I do this as well for onions. And if you thought that it was impressive that Heinz had "57 Varieties" (although they did have a few more, but Mr. Heinz just happened to like that number), there are more than six hundred varieties of garlic, and still counting.

Herbs

The most commonly used fresh herbs in Italy are oregano, thyme, bay leaf, marjoram, rosemary, and, of course, basil. Since herbs are mostly self-explanatory, or at least explained somewhere else, they need no further introduction from me. I will confine myself to where they have placed in my life. Fresh herbs were exclusively an anomaly in our house. Any herbs that found their way to our kitchen came dried in jars, and they mostly remained there until they were well out of date. In summer, however, there was never a shortage of fresh basil growing in my grandmother's vegetable garden. Fragrant, beautiful basil! When my parents bought the house from her in the mid-'70s (and kept her along with the garden), my mother continued the tradition. I loved basil's pungent yet slightly sweet aroma, but that was all I ever knew of it. All of that gorgeous basil was plucked, washed, and set out to dry or to be frozen. Looking back at the lackluster remains, I would conjecture that even the Egyptians knew better how to mummify the dead. I did not understand the miracle that basil was until I was in graduate school. Curiously, I had come upon it many years earlier without knowing it. In the Ian Fleming short story "Risico," James Bond orders "Tagliatelle Verdi with a Genoese sauce . . . which was improbably concocted from basil, garlic, and fir cones." *Pesto*, of course.

After learning how to make *pesto*, I snatched as much basil as I could before my mother could desecrate it. I doubt if a fortnight goes by in summer in which I don't add basil to a dish. But once upon a (happily distant) time, fresh basil was primarily a summer herb. Although nearly every supermarket carries fresh basil today, as little as twenty years ago it was difficult to find all year long. The first time I found some in a market in Old Greenwich, Connecticut, the cashier had no idea what it was or what you did with it.

Curiously, many Italians will tell you that it is extremely bad luck to cut rather than tear basil. Ask them why, and they will firmly tell you, *"Non lo so."* I don't know. Like so many bits of folkloristic advice, there is a practical side. It is not so much for poor luck as it is for poor taste. Cutting basil actually harms the plant, often turning it black. Quite simply, torn basil always tastes fresher and lasts longer. The autumn was upon me as I wrote this, and I am already longing for my own fresh basil with some olive oil and the now departed vine-ripened tomatoes

I think that the only other fresh herb I knew of was parsley. We did not use it, but apparently restaurants did, and for a purpose that had nothing in kinship with edibility. Parsley, and curly parsley at that, was strictly a garnish. I don't believe I was even ten when my mother scolded me in a Howard Johnson's restaurant for eating the sprig of parsley accompanying my open-faced turkey sandwich. Apart from parsley, (fresh) sage, rosemary, and thyme were merely words in a Simon and Garfunkel song. Today I have them all growing in my garden, and I believe I could indulge in cannibalism if rosemary was involved.

Olive Oil and Vinegar

Small bottles of olive oil were hardly economical for us in the 1960s, and extra-virgin olive was nonexistent. My mother opted for the three-liter can of oil, the contents of which had little to no flavor on its own. Why did we buy it? We were Italians; we had to, silly. In the same way that many Americans have never tasted real maple syrup, many still haven't a clue that olive oil can be anything but a urine-colored and "healthful" butter substitute (note well that there is no substitute for good butter). If there is one thing to be said for the can of olive oil that my mother bought, it did not make rhapsodic claims to being "nutty," "grassy," "fruity," and so on. I could not even postulate how the elder Giovanni "Gingi" (and don't ask me how to spell it) Carmello in his Corona establishment would have characterized such claims: "Nutty" would most assuredly have led the pack.

Unfortunately, as much as 50 percent of the olive oil sold in America is, to some degree, fraudulent. Some manufacturers intentionally mislead consumers into believing that the oil within the bottle is 100 percent Italian when it actually contains a blend of olives from different countries. Blended oils can be perfectly good—in fact, very good—and the better ones would never misrepresent themselves as 100 percent Italian. Shady dealers along the food supply chain frequently adulterate olive oil with low-grade vegetable oils and add artificial coloring. Given the growing glut of imposters, UNAPROL, the National Union of Olive Producers in Italy, has introduced the qualification "100 percent *Qualità Italiana*" as a new grade of extra-virgin olive oil in order to guarantee high quality. Independent tests at the University of California found that 69 percent of all store-bought extra-virgin olive oils in the United States are probably fake. This study found that Bertolli, Carapelli, Newman's Own, and Whole Foods failed to meet extra-virgin olive oil standards.

Real olive oil can be peppery and perky or subtle, buttery, and smooth. The flavor can be something individual to every person's taste. What isn't to every person's taste? The key to getting the best olive oil is to track down reviews, speak to people in specialty shops, and, whenever possible, taste before you buy. Also be mindful that California, Greece, France, and Spain produce superb cold-pressed oils. Actually, any country that can grow olives has the capacity to produce a fine olive oil. Although I am virtually hard-pressed to choose one brand over another, I have a partiality for oils from Sicily and Umbria that I buy at reasonable prices online from Fairway Market. Reliable, easy-to-find, and less-expensive brands are Columela from Italy, Pompeian, and California Olive Ranch.

As for vinegar, if you were to look for balsamic vinegar thirty years ago in most American towns, it would have been tantamount to Diogenes searching for an honest man. Balsamic is now the best-selling vinegar in America, accounting for 45 percent of all supermarket vinegar sales. The brands are so numerous that it is often a challenge to find plain red wine vinegar. If nearly everyone has heard of balsamic vinegar, not many people know that there are actually two kinds of balsamic vinegar made by entirely different processes. The time-honored technique by Italian law takes a minimum of ten to twelve years of aging in wooden casks; the modern industrial method may take as little as a few hours. The centuries-old traditional way usually begins with *only* the must of white Trebbiano grapes grown in Emilia-Romagna. Tradizionale di Modena vinegars, or *condimentos*, are packaged with the official seal of the Produttori Condimento (Consorzio Produttori) around the neck of the bottle. At the far end of the scale, a small bottle of fifteen- year-aged Acetaia Leonardi will run you about $100, but a scant drop or two will glorify a pork loin or a roast chicken. Heck, some people even sip it as a liqueur. If you are looking for something completely different, try a drop on a piece of 100 percent dark chocolate. For the inquisitive among you, the word "balsamic" is derived from "balm" because of the vinegar's purported medicinal properties, including its use in the past as a protection against the plague. So keep some handy—you never know.

With no law defining balsamic vinegar in the United States, manufacturers supply the huge demand in any way they can by coloring and sweetening wine vinegar and calling it "balsamic vinegar of Modena." *Read the label:* If the ingredients include red wine vinegar, it is not balsamic vinegar. Sadly, there are shifty companies that don't specify other ingredients, and almost anything could be in the bottle.

Fini and Lucini are reliable brands that won't demolish your pocket, and they are best used as a finishing drizzle over quality meats, cheeses, or fruits. The less expensive kind, such as the balsamic from Fairway at $6.99, is perfect in a salad dressing or marinade. At about $4 a bottle, a house brand like Trader Joe's can also adequately fit the cruet. Finally, don't neglect the red wine vinegar. It was and can still be an integral part of a good salad dressing.

Pasta and Rice

More will be said about pasta in its particular section, but suffice it to say that I did not have pasta growing up. We ate spaghetti or, sometimes, wagon wheels (*ruote di carro*). When it wasn't called spaghetti, it was macaroni. Either way, it was overcooked. "Al dente" was the name of an auto mechanic as far as my mother was concerned. "Spaghetti" may be translated as "little strings," and that would serve as an accurate description for what graced our table. As for other pasta I knew, lasagne and *ziti* were on their own terms because they disappeared amid the mounds of ricotta and meat sauce. Our "house" brand spaghetti was Ronzoni, although I preferred La Rosa. This was not because La Rosa was any better; it was because it just sounded better than Ronzoni. I later learned that the company was founded in 1914 by Vincenzo La Rosa, a Sicilian immigrant. When he noticed an increased demand for macaroni during World War I, he started making it in the back of his shop in Williamsburg, Brooklyn, and he became an innovator in the development of the packaged foods industry. Who would have thought?

A trip to a large market will demonstrate that there is clearly no shortage of dried or fresh pasta or pasta varieties and shapes. It is always good to stock up on a wide variety of pasta shapes. That way you will have choices to match your pasta with an appropriate sauce (I will go into pasta and sauce pairings, or toppings, in the respective recipes). There are worse things than going to your larder for a tubular pasta only to find spaghetti or linguine, but I cannot think of anything offhand. Regarding making home-made pasta, once you learn the technique, it is a fairly easy process. It is also a splendid and great way for the family to work together. The only draw-back is that you will need a pasta machine. But go ahead, you deserve it! By the way, if you ever see anyone break spaghetti in half, even if it's done by a dearest friend, break off the relationship immediately.

It is generally recognized that Marco Polo's bringing pasta to Italy is a fabulous myth. Even good old Marco in his accounts compares the noodles of China with the *vermicelli* of his own native Italy. Although pasta in its various forms had been known in Italy before he spoke about it, rice as a staple had not. Rice from Asia was mentioned as early as the first century in Pliny the Elder's *Natural History*, but it was recognized only for its medicinal properties. The earliest documented rice cultivation in Italy dates to 1475 in Lombardy, where its planting was promoted by Galeazzo Maria Sforza, the duke of Milan. Is it any surprise that the Milanese people are known for their *risotto*? Rice soon spread throughout the country, and Italy has become the biggest producer of rice in Europe. There are 3,000 known varieties of rice worldwide, and Italy produces 150 of them. Among the best-known are Arborio, Carnaroli, and Roma, and all are mainly used for *risotto*, while Originario and Padano are used in soups. Each type of rice has its proponents. The Carnaroli is less likely to get overcooked, but the harder-to-find Vialone Nano from Verona is smaller and therefore cooks faster and absorbs flavors better. We had but one variety in our house—Minute Rice.

Pepper and Peppers

Black pepper in our Queens residence was exactly the same vapid dust that one finds in little packets at fast-food emporiums. Saltpeter, one of the major constituents of gunpowder, is a preferable alternative. The only time I think I ever saw a real pepper mill was the four-foot one perched on a shelf of the Cinque Terre Italian restaurant in Flushing. It was set there just for display (and not too far from the four-foot bottle of Galliano). I know that I need not tell you how vital freshly ground pepper is, whether it is simply an embellishment to a green salad or an integral part of *Cacio e Pepe* (page 133). The basic problem is with most pepper mills. They are still more showy than serviceable. The grinder that makes my day is a Unicorn nine-inch Magnum-Plus, made in Nantucket, Massachusetts. I have had it for at least fifteen years, and it still grinds from very fine to coarse with ease. I also have their MiniMill, which is perfect for travel.

To some extent, one might regard crushed red pepper in the same way as ground pepper, particularly if you buy it already crushed. When I run out of my own dried peppers, I will buy whole red pepper pods and grind just enough to last a couple of weeks. The advantage of growing and drying your own peppers is that you can mix and match to acquire the level of heat you feel most comfortable with. Sniffing crushed red pepper should make you sneeze! If your crushed red pepper don't make you sneeze, it is time to get some more. As with the tomato, garlic, and olive oil, crushed red pepper, while used in the north, are more common to the southern part of Italy.

And now for a pet peeve: Have you ever noticed that the holes in red pepper shakers are invariably too small? It seems that whenever I go out for pizza I find that to be the case—even at the best pizzerias. Who knows how long that red pepper has been in there? I have given up mentioning this to the wait staff, as they pay no attention to me anyway ("Oh, please! Not another food *fascista!*") When I purchased my most recent shaker, I reamed out the holes a bit. That ensures that the pepper will be used in a timely fashion.

With respect to green or red bell peppers, they were never to be seen in our house when I was growing up. Italian frying peppers made a rare appearance when my father wanted peppers and eggs, but I am ashamed to say that I had not tasted a raw red sweet pepper until I was twenty-five. I was doing the best that I could with my European travel grant, but trying to get by on a dollar a day was a chore that managed to shed pounds off of me. There were moments when I thought I could eat a braised wombat. When I arrived in Germany, I met up with a friend who picked me up in his car on the way back from the market. He must have seen the saliva forming like lather around my mouth, and he asked me if I would like something to eat. He tossed me a red bell pepper. At the moment I think I could have shared a goat's dinner of barbed wire and broken beer bottles, and I chomped right in. I now grow ten varieties of hot and sweet peppers in my garden, and they don't remotely resemble barbed wire and broken beer bottles (except perhaps the "ghost" pepper, which is stupidly hot).

Lastly, I include the following bit of trivia only because there is a report that seems to be repeatedly popping up on food blogs. Peppers are also one way to boost your immunity and help prevent illness, but like everything else grown under the sun, peppers are not immune to at least something: myth. In case you haven't already heard this assertion, there is an allegation that peppers have a gender. The ones with four bumps are supposedly female and those with three bumps are male. The people who believe this are the same ones who eat carrots to improve their vision. If someone mentions this ridiculous flummery to you, merely tell him that the pepper is the fruit of the plant, and that it is the flower that contains the male and female genders (and offer him a carrot for his eyesight).

Salt

There was no such thing as a little salt in our house. Pouring on the salt was something we did unthinkingly, usually shaking it over our food even before we tasted it. My family found it quite amusing that I would put small mounds of salt on my plate in order to dip my meat. My teeth ache just recalling it. I was in high school when my friend Richard Cappuccio told me one way his father would size up prospective employees and evaluate them before hiring them. He would take them out to lunch to see how they would act in an informal situation. One criterion for immediately eliminating the potential new hire to his law firm was if he put salt on his food before tasting it. If the successful Mr. Cappuccio deemed this trivial act to be a mortal sin, there had to be something to it, and I most assuredly did not even ask for salt when I was invited over to their house for dinner.

Blood pressure notwithstanding, it would be folly to cook without salt. The ages have shown that a judicious use of salt will bring out the character of foods by not merely flavoring, but by stimulating our taste buds as well—and who can argue with the ages? When to add salt is a matter unto itself. For pasta, add salt just after the water comes to a boil—not before. Similarly, a sauce of fresh tomatoes will benefit with an early sprinkling because salt will help to break down the tomatoes while enhancing their essence. To the contrary, long-simmered dishes, like soups or stews, should be salted lightly at first. Adding salt too early will cause it to be absorbed too quickly by the vegetables, particularly potatoes. In fact, as a tip, if your soup is too salty, add a quartered potato: it will soak in much of the salty excess. Otherwise, taste your soup or stew toward the end of the cooking time on the stove and adjust the salinity then.

The great actor—and marvelous cook—Danny Kaye on salt: "There are two kinds of salt, salty salt and not so salty salt. I use the salty kind, sea salt." This is sage advice, and a simple matter to follow these days given the variety of sea salt available. Common sense tells us that the coarser the salt, the longer it will take to dissolve. In the best of all possible worlds, you should have at least two types to suit the occasion. At least one should be a kitchen staple: kosher salt. It will serve most of your needs admirably well. Be aware, though, that not all kosher salt is the same. I prefer Diamond Crystal to Morton, but if you choose the latter, note that it is heavier by volume. One cup of Morton salt weighs 8 ounces, while a cup of Diamond Crystal weighs 5 ounces (now you know why a box of the latter is larger, although it weighs the same as a package of Morton salt). For those keeping score, table salt weighs in at 10 ounces per cup. I often use sea salt (coarse, fine, or flakey, depending on what I'm using it for) when I cook, but all of the recipes herein will benefit equally from kosher salt unless otherwise specified.

Use your discretion when seasoning your meal after it is cooked. Overdoing the salt can make salt into a boisterous latecomer to a party who arrives just as everyone else is going, leaving a bad taste in your mouth. I have become so picky about adding salt to my cooking that I do not put salt on the table. Unlike freshly ground black or crushed red pepper, both of which add a new dimension to a particular dish, salt may not have time to dissolve properly. When I posted my opinion about this on a Web site many years ago, I was once again likened to a "food Nazi" deserving of tar and feathers. In my defense, I maintain, trust the cook. Consider it an insult to his or her cooking that you should be bold enough to try to improve upon it. If you would never dream of asking your host for some more carrots or beans for your soup, then pass on the salt, Walt.

Soffritto

While not a single ingredient, *soffritto* does serve as a "holy trinity," three being one. In Italian cooking, *soffritto* is the term used to describe the mix of chopped or diced onions, carrot, and celery. While I do not use the term in the recipes for this book, because the amounts of onion, carrot, and celery may vary according to the recipe, it is an important word to know. In French, it is *mirepoix*; and for the Spanish (who substitute tomato for celery), it is *sofrito*. By any other name, it is a basic building block for almost anything that can be cooked in a pot. So how could so essential a component of Italian cooking

*"Nanny" in her vegetable garden
in Queens, c.1950*

elude me until graduate school? Being self-taught would explain it, but I never once saw that mix of diced onion, carrot, and celery sautéing in butter or olive oil on our stove in my mother's kitchen. Onion, yes; celery or carrot, never. The very foundation of not only Italian, but so much of European cooking was AWOL from our home. In a word, it was missing because chopping was "work." But I have railed about the average American's aversion to that elsewhere. Even food pundit Michael Pollan, who loves to cook, hates to chop. As of this writing, there is no app for chopping yet.

Canned and Fresh Tomatoes

Tomatoes, like the use of olive oil versus butter, were something of a line of demarcation for Italy. The New World fruit took hold more in southern Italy, while the north preferred dishes without it. One reason for this is that the tomato, being a member of the deadly nightshade family, was thought to be poisonous. The Italians in Naples were so poor that they began chopping them and spreading them on bread to enhance their paltry daily fare. They also began cultivating a sweet variety that grew well in nearby San Marzano sul Sarno in Campania. Italians are not alone in believing that some of the best plum tomatoes in the world originated in San Marzano, but the word *pomodori* on the label does not an Italian tomato make.

Everyone is accustomed to that cluster of ripe, red tomatoes on the can and the accompanying words *pomodori pelati*. Many of us assume that they are Italian tomatoes. This is where the vigilant shopper must do his or her label reading again. Does the label say where the tomatoes are from? Where they were packed? Even if they are Italian, there is no guarantee that they are quality tomatoes. The only way to be sure of this is if somewhere on the can you see "San Marzano" as well as "imported from Italy." San Marzano growers are proud of the reputation of their tomatoes and will prominently display their distinction on their labels. That said, I should emphasize that our own California-grown organic tomatoes from Muir Glen are an excellent choice. Chef Chris Bianco and grower Rob DiNapoli have also teamed up to produce their own splendid organic Italian-style whole peeled tomatoes with basil in California: Bianco DiNapoli. If you cannot find Muir Glen canned tomatoes in your market, Amazon Pantry now offers them.

Shall I compare thee to a summer's day tomato? As for fresh tomatoes, I don't remember my first kiss (although it may have been from Bonnie Stern). I do however vividly recall my first bite into a newly picked tomato. It was in a neighbor's backyard. I was six years old, and I watched as Mr. Matinas plucked the juicy red orbs, sliced them in half, sprinkled them with salt, and proudly dispensed them to all the eager hands waving before him. Curious about the unanimous enthusiasm, I reached out and took one of the halves. It was a revelation as well as a joy that has not yet abated. My grandmother's garden teemed with tomatoes, but by the time they made it to our table, my mother had mixed them with chopped bits of iceberg lettuce and drenched it all in Wishbone Italian dressing. It wasn't long after my introduction to the fruit that freshly sliced beefsteak tomatoes (with salt, of course) became a part of nearly every summer meal.

I am fortunate enough to have the luxury of being able to plant my own tomatoes, and I usually grow about eighteen varieties, mostly heirlooms, of myriad shapes and colors. For those who don't have the land, time, or inclination, good summertime tomatoes are more widely available than ever. The local food movement, at least here in Western Massachusetts, has given rise to farmers' markets in nearly every community. You deal with the growers firsthand, and they know that if they do not make a good impression, you will not come back for more. Meanwhile, unlike coops, most supermarkets deal with suppliers, not growers. Despite their claims that they have the freshest produce, they probably do not. That cluster of beautiful, uniform red Holland tomatoes still on the vine may be more familiar than a gnarly

Cherokee Purple, but you don't taste with your eyes. The next time you are in a store buying tomatoes, try this simple, sneaky trick: As you pick up the tomato to sniff it, gently scratch it with your fingernail. If it does not smell like a fresh tomato, don't expect it to taste like one. In fact, don't expect it to taste like anything.

Happily, tomatoes take well to freezing if you are not up to canning. One way to store them is by blanching them for about 20 seconds or so and slipping off their skin. Then halve them and remove the seeds. Apportion them into small plastic bags, add a basil leaf, and seal tightly, removing all the air. As I mention in my recipe for *Long-Simmered Summer Tomato Sauce* (page 59), when the sauce is cool, spoon it into bags or flat plastic containers that will stack easily in the freezer. If using the latter, place a piece of plastic wrap atop the sauce, sealing it to prevent freezer burn. If you have a vacuum sealing system, all the better. Feel free to pour off any water that accumulates after defrosting.

As for sun-dried tomatoes, at least in this country, the term is a misnomer since most packaged varieties are dried in many ways besides basking in the sun. Some commercial sun-dried tomatoes, like other dried fruits, are treated with sulfur dioxide. Although sulfur dioxide is considered to be safe, some people are sensitive to it, particularly those who are prone to asthma. Apart from being a tasty addition to many dishes, sun-dried tomatoes keep their nutritional value (which includes antioxidants, vitamin C, and lycopene). Unlike loose sun-dried tomatoes, which have a long shelf life, those preserved in olive oil need to be refrigerated after opening. A fine layer of olive oil will also help preserve an open can of tomato paste. Since tomato paste is so rich, I tend not to use much of it at a time. This is where tubes of paste come in handy.

For trivia buffs: the tomato was thought to have been poisonous. It is technically a fruit and not a vegetable. In the late nineteenth century, imported vegetables were taxed, but not fruit. To garner extra revenue, in 1893 the U.S. Supreme Court affirmed that the tomato should be classified under customs regulations as a vegetable rather than a fruit. In fact, according to John Mariani in *How Italian Food Conquered the World*, the sixteenth-century botanist Piero Andrea Matiolli called tomatoes *pomi d' oro*—"golden apples." Whence comes the word itself, *pomodoro*. A fruit by any other name, as they say, is still a fruit. Nevertheless, as the saying goes, "Knowledge is knowing that a tomato is a fruit; wisdom is not putting it in a fruit salad."

Water

As unassuming as it may appear to be, I stress that water is indeed an ingredient, and this was one ingredient we always had in the house. It is sad to say, but it was not very good. Whether it was because of antiquated plumbing or fluoride in the water, our water tasted metallic and needed to sit for several minutes before the milky cloudiness dissipated. If I were to take a stab at playing Bill Nye "the Science Guy," it is that the old pipes were thin and caked with minerals, thereby causing more pressure and tiny air bubbles as a result. Our ice was almost as white as my uncle Jim's new dentures. The popularity of bottled water was still decades away, and for drinking there were the old reliable seltzer bottles, which were delivered by the case every week. (Today, a single antique seltzer bottle on eBay can go for the equivalent of half a year's supply of full cases, in case you were wondering.)

As it was back then so it is today, many people who would never drink funky water don't think twice about making ice or cooking with it. Just as ice made from bad water will ruin a cocktail, sufficiently rank water will impart its taste to cooked food. I recently stayed in a house in Vermont where the water was so abysmal that I was even apprehensive about showering in it, let alone cooking with it. Fortunately, most of the water in our homes is not so foul that boiling will not serve to remedy this.

So how is water an ingredient? For soups and braises, the answer seems glaringly apparent. Even if you start with wine or stock, as Michael Pollan points out, these liquids are really just enhanced forms of water, H_2O serving as what chemists call the "continuous phase" in which various other molecules disperse to great and flavorful effect. Science aside, let us say that you start a soup or braise with a liquid of choice. As your dish cooks down, and too much red wine, say, is absorbed or evaporated, the result promises to be dry or even burnt food. Do you add more wine? Certainly not. The wine will be raw, unlike the wine that mellowed over the slow cooking. White wine, though, is more forgiving. If you started with beef stock, should you add more? Not necessarily. Although the stock may not have the acidity or rawness of red wine, it may not have the time to blend with the other ingredients. It could be more like an intruder offering a new and different dimension of its own. The best answer is water, as it will simply revitalize the cooked-down liquids. Think of a cup of tea that is too strong because you forgot to take out the tea bag. What do you add? Water.

Similarly, if your sauce has become too dense, whether it is a tomato sauce or a purée such as *pesto*, add a bit of water to loosen it to a desired consistency. When making a dish with *pesto*, I always add a dollop of *pesto* and a splash of hot pasta cooking water and blend them before I add the pasta and the rest of the *pesto*. I find that this gives the dish a silky edge. "Crude" pasta sauces, such as those with asparagus or broccoli sautéed briefly in garlic and olive oil, will benefit from this, too, as the hot cooking water helps deglaze the pan, thus enhancing the flavor of the dish.

Water also plays an essential role in several Roman dishes, such as *Cacio e Pepe* and *Spaghetti con Aglio, Olio, e Peperoncino*. The key ingredient in those dishes is the cooking water. When you use the right amount of pasta water, you have a thick and round and rich sauce the Romans call a cremina. Add too much too quickly, however, and you might as well have ordered Chinese takeout instead.

Sauces and Stocks

One of the very nicest things about life is the way we must regularly stop whatever it is we are doing and devote our attention to eating.

—LUCIANO PAVAROTTI

More often than not, my mother's sauce was a murky mess. I should emphasize "sauce" (pronounced *sawce*), because unlike other Italian American families, we never referred to it as "gravy." Gravy was viscous brown stuff that you poured into the sinkhole of your instant mashed potatoes. The product of a long simmering process, tomato sauce was spawned from purée, occasionally crushed canned tomatoes, or, by mistake, whole canned tomatoes. To this salmagundi she snuck in a jar or can of Italian-style tomato sauce, I suspect to spare herself the chore of chopping onions or garlic. Come to think of it, I do not recall ever seeing my mother chop an onion with a knife. She did have a cylindrical plastic gadget with something of a plunger on top and blades within. It was fairly worthless, as half the onion lodged itself on the blades and the rest was ground to a tear-invoking pulp.

Once the sauce was on the stove, the simmering would go on for hours, the sauce bubbling away, not so much to develop flavor—a chimera at best—but because that was what you were supposed to do. Thus, as the sauce was bound to become bitter, my mother would add copious amounts of salt, sprinkles of sugar, and dashes of a nebulous ingredient called Italian seasoning in an attempt to revive and to revitalize it—to resurrect it from the dead, as it were. On that account, if she were the Lord, Lazarus would never have gotten his second wind. Dead was dead in my mother's saucepot.

I rarely long-simmer a tomato sauce, except in the summertime from garden-fresh tomatoes. This sauce is then frozen to be served during the winter months when a lush, ripe tomato is a precious commodity. When I do make a sauce with canned tomatoes, I like to get my hands into it—literally. A New York firefighter told me that to truly be the "owner" of your sauce, you must crush your tomatoes by hand. First pour the tomato liquid from the can into your pot, and then gradually crush the tomatoes, pouring more liquid into the pot as you go. As each tomato is broken apart, drop it into the sauce. You may also discard some of the harder core pieces if you like, but I do not. Canned tomatoes need only be cooked until their liquid has started to evaporate and incorporate itself with the other ingredients. This will depend on the density and water and fat contents of your other ingredients, but the time required will be from 25 to 45 minutes. Clearly, lowering the heat to a minimum will allow more time if the family is still lingering over their cocktails.

Red wines are ideal for long-simmered beef and meat stews and braises, yet a delicate veal dish such as *ossobuco* benefits greatly from a white wine. I have found that white wine is used far more extensively than red in Italian cooking. Having worked in an award-winning restaurant, I learned that one need not pour your money into the pot with the *vino*. There are many crisp, dry whites for under $10 that will work admirably.

And remember, as I stated earlier, water is an ingredient. If your tomato sauce has begun to cook down too quickly, you are not so much adding water as you are replacing what has evaporated. On that note, I hope I am not belaboring the aforementioned, but the tomato is a New World fruit. Prior to explorers' visits to the Americas, the tomato was unknown in Europe. A typical example of an old-world sauce that is still being made is for *pasta alla Genovese.* This is a long-simmered sauce of basically braised beef and plenty of onions, topped with cheese.

The reason that the sauces in this section are not paired with pasta is not whimsical. I find that these sauces are so versatile that they can be paired with any number of pastas, or even other dishes entirely. You could just as easily serve the *Spicy Raw Tomato Sauce with Garlic and Basil* with spaghetti as with fusilli or on pizza or steak *Pizzaiola.* It is also important not to over-sauce a dish so that the pasta is submerged and forgotten. The sauce and pasta should embrace each other. And, as I mentioned previously, it is good to stock up on a wide variety of pasta shapes so you have the right pasta to match the appropriate sauce.

Spicy Raw Tomato Sauce with Garlic and Basil

MAKES APPROXIMATELY 4 SERVINGS

I could eat this sauce with pasta at least once a week when tomatoes are in season. This single dish tells me that summer is finally in full bloom. If you are like my wife, and are especially sensitive to raw garlic, I would recommend sautéing it in a little bit of olive oil just until it has lost its rawness. Do not let the garlic brown, as this will make the sauce bitter. I find, however, that when you let the sauce sit for a while, the garlic seems to "cook" in the acidity of the tomatoes. I have seen versions of this recipe that call for all of the ingredients to be put into a food processor—and I have wept profusely. Most recipes, even when not desecrating the tomatoes, add the basil at the beginning. To my mind, with this approach the basil loses some of its natural pepperiness and brilliant color; so I add half at the beginning and the rest toward the end. Also, if you have the time, let the sauce marinate for a couple of hours. This is one of the few instances where I would add salt early on in a recipe with fresh tomatoes. Salt will draw the juice out of a tomato, which is fine in this case, but could be a problem when you are serving fresh slices or chunks as part of an appetizer.

If you happen to have large shells and fresh mozzarella on hand, try this: As soon as you pour the hot pasta in the bowl, top it with a handful of diced fresh mozzarella. The cheese will melt just enough to add a creamy dimension to the dish. In this respect it is something of a *Caprese* pasta. If you grew your own tomatoes or paid dearly for them at a farmers' market, you have made an investment. You owe it to yourself, and the tomatoes, to find a bottle of the best quality olive oil for your summer dishes. Young fruity wines, like Dolcetto, are my choices to accompany fresh tomato dishes.

1 teaspoon minced young garlic cloves, or to taste
1 to 1½ pounds ripe tomatoes, seeded and coarsely chopped
¼ cup julienned or ¼-inch torn pieces fresh basil
3 tablespoons very good, grassy extra-virgin olive oil
½ teaspoon of coarse sea salt or kosher salt
Freshly ground black pepper to taste
1 pound of your favorite pasta
Freshly grated Parmigiano for serving

1. Combine the garlic, tomatoes, half the basil, olive oil, and salt and pepper in a large bowl and let them stand to marinate for at least 30 minutes or up to 2 hours.

2. When the sauce is done marinating, bring 4 quarts of water to a boil. Salt the water, add the pasta, and cook until al dente. Drain the pasta thoroughly and add it to the sauce with the remaining basil. Serve immediately with the Parmigiano.

Long-Simmered Summer Tomato Sauce

MAKES APPROXIMATELY 2 QUARTS

This is a lifesaver. I make batches of it and freeze it to use in recipes when fresh tomatoes are no longer available. As in all of my fresh tomato sauces, I prefer to use any number of heirloom and other tomatoes in lieu of paste tomatoes. I find that most paste tomatoes do not have the sparkle of other varieties. These garden tomatoes are sweeter and certainly need no sugar added to them. In short, for this recipe I cook only with the tomatoes that I would eat raw. The ingredients here are few because I use this as a jumping-off point for other sauces. In effect, although it could be served as is, this sauce is basically a tomato purée. This recipe is also a template and may be doubled or tripled if you have a bumper crop and a pot big enough to hold them. You do not need to add the tomatoes all at once. I actually prefer to cut several tomatoes at a time and add the fresh batches to the tomatoes that are already simmering.

¼ cup extra-virgin olive oil

1 cup coarsely chopped onion

½ teaspoon crushed red pepper

1 tablespoon coarsely chopped fresh garlic

3 pounds of fresh, ripe tomatoes

2 teaspoons coarse sea salt or kosher salt

1. In a large pot over medium heat, drizzle in the olive oil. Toss in the onion and cook, stirring, until just soft, about 3 minutes. Add the crushed red pepper and garlic and cook for another minute or so. Do not let the garlic brown. Meanwhile, start cutting the tomatoes into quarters, if medium, and eighths if large. Discard as much of the seeds as possible.

2. Add the tomatoes in batches as you cut them. As the tomatoes come to a boil, lower the heat and simmer uncovered for about 2 hours. Stir occasionally to help break up the tomatoes.

3. When the tomatoes have cooled just a little, place them through a food mill over another pot that will hold them. (If you do not have another large pot, purée the tomatoes over a bowl and return them to the original pot.) Discard the skins and whatever seeds remain. Return the sauce to the heat, add the salt, and simmer for another half an hour, stirring occasionally.

4. When the sauce is cool, spoon it into freezer bags or flat plastic containers that will stack easily in the freezer. If using the latter, place a piece of plastic wrap atop the sauce, sealing it to prevent freezer burn.

April Tomato Sauce

MAKES APPROXIMATELY 2 QUARTS

Why April, you ask? Usually by that time, no matter how much I make, all of my summer tomato sauce is gone, and life would not be worth living without a supply of sauce. For this sauce I use canned tomatoes, usually Muir Glen plum tomatoes. Pomì brand or other puréed tomatoes are serviceable alternatives in a pinch. Some authors slip in some sugar to their basic tomato sauce. Good tomatoes are naturally sweet, and if you have quality tomatoes, sugar is completely unnecessary, if not unthinkable. This recipe is similar to the above, but should take about half the time. As an alternative to puréeing tomatoes, coarsely chop them and use an immersion blender at the end of the cooking time. This will also render a thicker sauce.

¼ cup extra-virgin olive oil

1 cup finely chopped onion

½ cup finely chopped carrot

½ cup finely chopped celery

½ teaspoon crushed red pepper

1 tablespoon coarsely chopped fresh garlic

2 28-ounce cans good-quality tomatoes, preferably plum, puréed

2 teaspoons coarse sea salt or kosher salt

1. In a large pot over medium heat, drizzle in the olive oil. Toss in the onion and cook, stirring, until just soft, about 3 minutes. Add the carrot, celery, crushed red pepper, and garlic and cook for another minute or so. Pour in the tomatoes with their juice. Season with salt. Lower heat and simmer partially covered for from 45 minutes to an hour.

2. As above, when the sauce is cool, spoon it into freezer bags or flat plastic containers that will stack easily in the freezer. If using the latter, place a piece of plastic wrap atop the sauce, sealing it to prevent freezer burn.

Morel Mushroom Sauce with Pancetta

MAKES APPROXIMATELY 4 SERVINGS

I had always known that there was something remarkable about mushrooms. What I did not know in my early youth was that there were mushrooms that did not come in a can or a jar. As a young teenager, I was a big fan of Roger Moore as Simon Templar, *The Saint* (but never as James Bond). It was a ritual for me to sit in

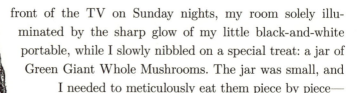

front of the TV on Sunday nights, my room solely illuminated by the sharp glow of my little black-and-white portable, while I slowly nibbled on a special treat: a jar of Green Giant Whole Mushrooms. The jar was small, and I needed to meticulously eat them piece by piece—stem first—and the cap—in order to savor them throughout the hour-long show. The other types of mushrooms we had in the house were marinated and served in an antipasto, sliced in a can of Franco-American gravy, or chopped into bits in Campbell's Cream of Mushroom Soup. I eventually did see the basket of typical white button mushrooms in the supermarket, but we never bought them. In fact, when I was teaching in New York in the early '80s, I bought an entire basket from a street vendor, but apart from putting them in a salad, I had no idea what to do with them.

I was giving an exam that day, and I offered my students extra credit if they could provide me with a recipe. The most original was a mushroom and spinach salad.

Commercially, the mushroom and its many varieties and uses have come a long way. In my restaurant days we had a fellow stop by once a week during wild mushroom season with a horde of morels, chanterelles, black trumpets, and other magnificent fungi. There was no need to ask him where he found them, because I am sure he would rather have had his tongue pried out with fireplace tongs than tell. The remarkable thing about some mushrooms is that after they are dried, they can come back to life with a greater vividness and a more concentrated flavor than they had when they were fresh. The reason for this in the case of fresh morels is that unless you prepare them the day they are picked, they will have lost their character en route to your specialty market. The ridged shape of morels also makes it imperative to wash the dried mushrooms thoroughly to rid them of the gritty bits hiding in the crevices. Another plus of the reconstituted morel, apart from being cheaper than fresh, is that they yield a "broth" in the bargain. The following versatile sauce can be paired well with any number of fresh pastas, from *pappardelle* to ravioli. If you cannot find dried morels, you can substitute a good quality porcini mushroom. With cream-based sauces some people prefer white wines, such as Pinot Grigio or a buttery Chardonnay, but I prefer a young Chianti or a Malbec. Hey, I'm a red wine person.

2 cups chicken stock or broth

2 ounces dried morel mushrooms

3 tablespoons unsalted butter

⅓ cup finely chopped shallots

3 ounces *pancetta*, finely diced

¼ teaspoon each coarse or kosher salt and freshly ground white pepper

1 cup heavy cream

¼ cup fresh flat-leaf parsley, coarsely chopped, plus more for sprinkling

1 pound fresh egg or stuffed pasta of your choice

Freshly grated Parmigiano for serving

1. Heat the stock until it comes to a soft rolling boil. Place the morels in a bowl and pour the stock over them, making sure they are completely submerged (a ramekin or other small bowl may help with this). Let the morels soak for 30 minutes. Strain the mixture through a fine-mesh sieve or cheesecloth and gently squeeze the soaking liquid from the morels. Set the strained liquid aside. Rinse the mushrooms until they are completely free of any grit. Slice them in half lengthwise and then in ¼-inch half-moons.

2. In a skillet large enough to accommodate the pasta, melt the butter over medium heat. Stir in the shallots and the *pancetta* and sauté until the *pancetta* just begins to brown, about 5 minutes. Add the mushroom liquid, stirring occasionally, and cook over low heat until reduced by half.

3. Stir in the salt and pepper and the heavy cream. Whisk gently until the mixture thickens, about 5 minutes. Blend in the morels and parsley. Cook and stir until heated through.

4. While the sauce is cooking, bring 4 quarts of water to a boil. Salt the water, add the pasta, and cook until al dente. Drain the pasta, reserving 1/4 cup pasta water, and add the pasta to the sauce.

5. Raise the heat to medium and toss the pasta to coat, about 1 minute. Use some of the pasta water *only* if the sauce seems to be too thick. Serve immediately and pass the Parmigiano and extra parsley.

Gorgonzola Sauce

MAKES APPROXIMATELY 4 SERVINGS

Gorgonzola shares a trait with almost all blue cheese. You love it or hate it. I know someone who cannot be in the same room with it—but we are still friends. I don't recall when I first tasted Gorgonzola. I certainly should have, it was such a revelation. And I am sure it was the harder, more crumbly variety rather than the buttery, unctuous Gorgonzola *dolce* I have come to love in a sauce. The two basic varieties of this marvelous blue-veined cheese differ mainly in their age. The younger is Gorgonzola *dolce* (sweet Gorgonzola), and the riper, more aged cheese is Gorgonzola *piccante* (also called mountain Gorgonzola). Although the latter seems more akin to blue cheese in its firmness, Gorgonzola is more typically made from unskimmed cow's milk while other blue cheese is made from the milk of sheep or goats.

GORGONZOLA DOLCE

As it is with so many Italian foodstuffs, the name "Gorgonzola" is protected by law and can only be produced in parts of Piedmont and

Lombardy in northern Italy. Since Italy's laws on food production do not apply outside the country's borders, you will find (mostly inferior) non-Italian brands in most supermarket cheese sections. I have so far encountered none that can compare with true Gorgonzola. The younger *dolce*, with its melting properties, makes an ideal and versatile sauce for any number of filled pastas as well as *gnocchi* or *risotto* (see *Spring Risotto with Gorgonzola, Ramps, and Cherry Tomatoes*, page 113). Apart from the savory flavor *dolce* imparts, what makes it especially appealing is that it is so simple to use in making a sauce.

> 4 tablespoons unsalted butter
> 1 cup heavy cream
> 6 ounces Gorgonzola *dolce*
> ½ cup freshly grated Parmigiano, plus more for serving
> Freshly ground black pepper to taste
> Coarse sea salt or kosher salt (optional)
> Filled pasta such as *tortellini*, *cappelletti*, ravioli, or *gnocchi*

Melt the butter in a saucepan large enough to hold the pasta or *gnocchi*. Add the cream to warm, but not boil. Crumble in the Gorgonzola and mash with the back of a wooden spoon. Stir until the cheese is well blended, about 5 minutes. Add the pepper and Parmigiano. Cook pasta as directed, blend in the sauce, and serve immediately, passing the extra Parm and black pepper.

Basic Stock

I am taking a great liberty here in assuming that not everyone has a reliable recipe for stock—or has even taken the bothersome time to make one. You may very well have your own favorite beef or chicken stock recipe, but not everyone does. If you do not have the time to make homemade stock, Better Than Bouillon and Minor's Beef Base are suitable alternatives. The former brand, in fact, makes half a dozen varieties of concentrated bases. Pound for pound, or ounce per ounce, these concentrates are excellent economical shortcuts. Ada Boni in her esteemed *Il Talismano della Felicità* even uses *brodo di dadi* in a pinch: bouillon cubes!

But if you do decide to go whole hog (but preferably beef or chicken), here is some rudimentary advice. First of all, don't throw away "dem bones." Freeze any leftover beef and veal bones or chicken and turkey carcasses. Adding any leftover bones to the fresh bones in the recipe below after the fresh bones have browned will enhance the flavor of your stock. Bear in mind that this is a basic recipe for either chicken or beef stock. Think of it as a guideline. You will need to correct the seasoning as the stock cooks down. Only you will know when the stock is to your taste. Once you have your stock, you may cook it down even further for a demi-glace. Containers of stock will last for a week refrigerated and for six months in the freezer. When freezing, store some in larger jars or tubs for soups or stews, but freeze some in individual containers or in ice cube trays for other, more moderate uses such as sauces or beefy Bloody Mary mixes.

For beef stock: 4 pounds beef bones, cut into 3-inch pieces
For chicken stock: 3 to 4 pounds chicken carcasses cut into
   pieces, along with giblets

2 each large carrots, onions, and celery ribs, roughly chopped
1 cup boiling water
8 quarts water
3 large fresh garlic cloves in their skins, lightly smashed
1 herb sachet (10 black peppercorns, 2 bay leaves, 4 sprigs
   fresh parsley, and 2 sprigs fresh thyme, or ½ teaspoon dried,
   tied in a piece of cheesecloth)
Salt to taste

1. Preheat your oven to 450 degrees. Spread the bones out in a large roasting pan to form a single layer. Roast for 15 minutes, turning occasionally. Add the vegetables and continue roasting, until the vegetables are brown, about 15 minutes.

2. Transfer the roasted bones and vegetables to a suitable size stockpot. Pour off the remaining fat from the roasting pan, set it on the stove over medium heat, and add the boiling water. Scrape the caramelized bits in the bottom of the pan and incorporate them into the boiling water. Add the cooking juices to the pot along with the rest of the ingredients.

3. Bring the liquid to a boil and immediately turn the heat to low. Simmer the stock for 4 to 5 hours, skimming the grayish scum off the top as the stock cooks.

4. Remove the stock from the heat and allow it to cool. Over a large bowl, strain the stock through a colander lined with cheesecloth. Refrigerate the stock overnight. After the stock has rested, the excess fat will have risen to the top and can be easily scraped off.

5. Transfer the cooled stock into suitable containers (described above) and refrigerate or freeze.

"Sandwiches again!"

❦

That phrase was originally uttered in a 1970s TV commercial by a fellow as he sat down to yet another dinner of sandwiches on white bread. His sullen wife apologized for having to make ends meet on the little income they had. The ad was for Driver Training Institute, and it assured you that you could make good money (up to $595 a week) as a driver if you had proper training—and without a high school degree. We never learned what they ate after he got the new job, though. Seeing that we lived over a Laundromat in an eighty-eight-dollar-a-month, two-bedroom sneaker box, our family of four was also on a very tight budget. Sandwiches were more the norm than pasta. There were always bundles of cold cuts wrapped in tin foil filling one of our refrigerator drawers: bologna, yellow American cheese, hard (not Genoa) salami, and my favorite, Boar's Head ham. I would come in for lunch and devour nearly an entire loaf of Italian bread stuffed with ham and cheese and slathered with Gulden's Spicy Brown Mustard.

Our meals of sandwiches were not strictly born out of necessity. They were hardly what you would call labor-intensive, sparing my mother any undue work. No, cooking was not a labor of love for my mother; it was just plain labor. The comedian Carrie Snow declared that she preferred Hostess fruit pies to Pop-Tarts because they required less cooking. That was my mother in a pie-crust shell. The early 1960s was a

My, but that boy could eat!

time when many stay-at-home moms, like my mother, were spared the trouble of chopping vegetables to make a soup from scratch. Besides, how could homemade compare with my favorite soup, Campbell's Cream of Mushroom? I know that I was not the only picky kid in America, and it must have been quite the relief when TV dinners began to line the freezer section of our King Kullen. My mother could now cheaply feed our finicky family four unique meals if need be, and please everyone in the bargain—and in no time at all. Convenience foods are vital to many workaholics today; it is just a matter of saving time. It may be extreme to follow Jim Harrison's blunt advice, "If you don't have an hour to cook your dinner quit your job," but he does deliver the wake-up call that we owe more to our families than a few minutes to provide for our sustenance.

Even when my mother worked at it, her best attempts paled in taste by comparison with the canned and packaged foods she bought. Italian essayist and author Umberto Eco has succinctly summed up the error of our ways: "Americans are spectacular at imitating the genuine, and in this case it is more profitable to imitate genuine food than produce it." Moreover, my mother completely bought into the commercial food industry's promise of economical, easily prepared meals. And so did I. As a kid, I fancied myself a "big guy" finishing off an entire Swanson Hungry Man dinner, which boasted of a slab of broiled Salisbury steak in gravy, accompanied by whipped potatoes, peas "in a seasoned sauce," chicken noodle soup, and the sugary wad of brown that passed itself off as dessert. Given the paucity of its nutritional value, "Swan Song" might have been more fitting, but I was hooked. Not that the commercial food industry and its advertising did not help to lure me in. One afternoon while watching TV, I was fascinated by an advertisement that flaunted a burly golden-haired Viking who clutched the ship's rigging with one hand and lustily chomped on a hunk of bread slathered with margarine in the other hand. It was so tantalizing that I begged my mother to buy some. One bite was enough for me. Right now I imagine that the uneaten three and a half sticks of the oleaginous stuff are going through the half-life process in some landfill somewhere. I mean, how can anything go bad that was never good in the first place?

Soups, Salads, Sides, and So Forth

Worries go down better with soup.

— JEWISH PROVERB

Multiple choice: A? B? C? D? In our house some of our meals were often unfathomable combinations of "All of the above." Dinner was also something of a race. It began exactly at 6:00 and ended by 6:15. With the fare as uninteresting as it usually was, it was a "giggle, gobble, and git" affair. For me the expediency was so that I could go outside and play. This irked my father no end. He may not have been enraptured over the greens and grays on his plate, but he had this concept called "family time." Baseball or hide-and-seek seemed far more appealing to a ten-year-old boy.

As it was with so many Italians, family was important to my father. If he was bothered when I moved out of the house, I don't think he ever forgave me for moving to Massachusetts. He never visited our home under the pretext that there was no one to take care of his dog. When the dog died, he then argued that he could not visit because he did not want to leave his house unguarded.

As I mentioned earlier, everything we were to eat came out at the same time. This meant that by the end of the meal, any bits left on your dish became a soup in its own right. Salad dressing, mushroom gravy, shards of Minute Rice, and whatever other dregs remained on the plate congealed into something between a late Jackson Pollock and an oil slick on the East River. If the origin of life was a primordial soup, this was more a depiction of its demise.

Speaking of soup, you say "po-tay-to" and I say "po-tah-to," as the song goes, but the Italians say *minestre, minestrone,* and *zuppe. Minestre* comes from the Latin ministrare, "to administer." This is because minestra was served out of a large pot by the head of the household. Minestra was usually the only course of the meal, and definitely *cucina povera*: peasant food. *Minestrone* is typically a denser dish due to thickening vegetables such as potatoes, carrots, or squash. It will also often include beans, pasta, or rice. If *minestra* was the soup of the poor, *zuppa* was for the poorest. It was basically just a homemade broth served with stale bread in it. The word itself derives from "soaked" bread. During the Middle Ages, the wealthy ate their meals on trenchers, or slabs of bread. The bread, which ended up saturated with the juices of meats and other foods, was sometimes sold to the poor, but more often it was given to the servants of the house. They in turn boiled the sopping bread in water or stock for their own meal: Soup was on for the other 99 percent!

So let us take our heading *Soup* first. Because it was so easily prepared right out of the can, soup was never served for dinner in our home. It was always lunch. It might have been served with a sandwich, but generally not. Then on to *Salad*. Our salad was a lesson in sogginess. As for *Sides*, they were partners in crime with the main course: meat (and almost always meat, except for Fridays, meat no-nos for Catholics then, and Lent). In the end, most of our meals lapsed into the *and So Forth* category. I hope the following recipes redress those lapses.

Minestrone with Pesto

SERVES 6 TO 8

W hat was it that made Campbell's Minestrone the vegetable soup of choice for us? Was it the MSG, the caramel coloring, or the 900 milligrams of sodium (40 percent of your daily value)? To a great extent it was the salt, to which I undoubtedly added more. But, being the universal noodle lover that I was (and am), it was more likely the *vermicelli*. The word *vermicelli* is derived from the Latin root *"vermin"* for "wormlike," and that is pretty much how I now view those squishy little noodles. If I may hazard a guess, I believe that this was the brew that the three witches were double-double-toiling-and-troubling in *Macbeth*. I look back in near horror at that viscous swamp of a soup with more "non-vegetable" ingredients than vegetables. I eventually learned that there was a use for Parmigiano cheese rinds—besides strengthening your teeth. They will enrich the soup while it is cooking. The trend for using the once-discarded rinds in soups has become so popular that even supermarkets have begun to carry them. Make sure you have enough, because your family may fight over them.

As I mentioned earlier, if you do not have homemade stock, there are serviceable, economical shortcuts. If making this soup may sound like quite a bit of work for just two people, it freezes well and will be there for that night when you come home late and don't have the time to cook. Unlike many other dishes, minestrone is quite malleable. After you sauté your *soffritto* of onions, carrot, and celery, you may add or subtract vegetables to suit your taste. If you are not a devotee of squash, add more beans, and so on. As Pellegrino Artusi avers in his *La scienza in cucina* (1891): "After making three tests and improving on it each time, this is the way I would make minestrone. You are free to modify it according to the customs of your particular part of the country and vegetables one finds there." Be it known that there is a tendency to serve minestrone as a first course in Italian restaurants in the United States, before a second course of pasta. This would be an anomaly in Italy because minestrone is a heavy soup, considered quite filling in its own right.

As a curious aside, Pellegrino Artusi went to a restaurant in Livorno to have dinner. After eating minestrone, he would later recount that he spent the whole night suffering from horrible stomach pains. He blamed them on the minestrone he had eaten. The next day, returning to Florence, he got the news that Livorno had been hit by cholera. It was only then that he realized what had happened: It had not been the minestrone that had made him ill, but the early symptoms of the disease. The event inspired Artusi to write the earliest known recipe for minestrone, which includes *pancetta* and pork rind. He warns that it is not a soup for weak stomachs! Have no fear here.

½ cup olive oil

2 cups halved and thinly sliced yellow onions

½ teaspoon crushed red pepper

1 cup scrubbed and diced carrots

1 cup de-stringed and diced celery (use a peeler for de-string-ing if you like)

1 yellow summer squash and 1 zucchini, ends removed and diced (about 2 cups)

5 to 6 ounces green beans, stems removed, cut into 1-inch pieces (about 1 cup)

2 cups diced potatoes, peeled (or unpeeled if scrubbed and relatively smooth)

1 small Savoy or Napa cabbage, quartered, cored, and shred-ded (about 4 cups)

1 28-ounce can whole peeled tomatoes, hand-crushed

8 cups homemade beef broth (or the equivalent from concen-
trate; see previous recipe for stock)
Several Parmigiano cheese rinds to taste
Freshly ground pepper and coarse or kosher salt to taste
2 15.5-ounce cans cannellini beans, drained
Freshly grated Parmigiano cheese for serving
Pesto for serving (recipe follows)

1. Begin by slicing the onions. A mandoline helps here. Heat the oil in a large stockpot over medium-low heat. Add the onions and crushed red pepper and resume preparing the rest of the vegetables. Once the onion begins to soften, about 4 minutes, stir in the diced carrots for another 2 minutes. Repeat this process in about 2-minute intervals with the celery, squash, zucchini, green beans, and potatoes, stirring as you go. Last, add the cabbage and cook for about 5 minutes, stirring occasionally.

2. Start pouring the tomato liquid into your pan, and then quickly crush the tomatoes and add them to the sauce. Add the broth and the cheese rinds. Add water, if necessary, to cover the vegetables. Cover and simmer over low heat until the soup thickens, about 3 hours. During the last half hour, add the pepper and taste and season with salt as needed.

3. Fifteen minutes before the soup is done, add the canned beans. Serve each portion with a piece of cheese rind, and pass the grated cheese and *pesto*.

Pesto

MAKES APPROXIMATELY 4 SERVINGS

I mentioned earlier that despite the bushels of fresh basil we had every summer, my mother would dry it—or worse, try to freeze it. The outcome of the latter process resembled a durable roofing material. I have brought my mother fresh basil every year since the time she was no longer able to grow it. I did make it a point to leave before I saw the method she was going to use to defile it. I was always content to make my pesto in a blender, as the amount of pesto I whipped up every year would require a cauldron instead of a mortar. It was also so easy and quick that I had no need to return to the original method of grinding it by hand. Therefore, I did not foresee what the fates would deal me in France.

My wife, Valdina, and I were staying with her parents in an art dealer's apartment on the Seine overlooking the Louvre. Her parents had invited some important rare book dealers over for dinner, and I, being the family cook, was asked to prepare it. "Why not your wonderful *pesto* as a first course?" my mother-in-law suggested. We were right around the corner from a superb open-air market, and I was able to procure all of the ingredients, save for the fresh cheeses. I don't know if it was national pride, or chauvinism, but the only Parmigiano I could muster came already grated in tiny bags. It would have to do. What I particularly did not account for was that the art dealer was a *célibataire*: a bachelor. There was no food processor, no blender, and now I was up the proverbial creek with no paddle or processor. Frantically looking around, I spied a sixteenth-century Venetian mortar and pestle bedecking one of his shelves. I am pleased to say that I have made *pesto* the traditional way—but only once, thank goodness!

Butter is fairly common in *pesto* these days, but it was not part of the earlier recipes. For a smokier touch, toast the pine nuts first. The uses for *pesto* are many, but I would highly recommend *Trennete al Pesto*. The pasta is blended not only with the *pesto* but also with cooked potatoes and sometimes green beans. I like to add sun-dried tomatoes as well.

2 to 3 cups tightly packed fresh basil leaves

1½ teaspoons chopped garlic

⅓ cup pine nuts

½ cup the best extra-virgin olive oil, and more as needed

1 teaspoon salt

3 tablespoons freshly grated Parmigiano cheese

3 tablespoons freshly grated Pecorino Romano

1 teaspoon salt

A pinch of finely ground black pepper

2 tablespoons unsalted butter, softened (optional)

1. Combine the basil, garlic, pine nuts, olive oil, and salt in a food processor or blender, and pulse a few times until evenly blended. You may need to scrape down the bowl with a spatula from time to time. Pulsing is preferable here, because running the food processor or blender continuously may overheat the mixture. Add more oil as needed.

2. When the ingredients are fully incorporated, transfer the mixture to a bowl and blend in the cheeses. Lastly, blend in the softened butter, if so desired.

Cardoon Soup with Garlic Croutons

SERVES 4

We certainly never made this unusual soup in my house when I was a kid, and I am equally certain that most people in this country haven't either. First, you would need to know what cardoons are. Secondly, you would need to know where to buy them. Happily, this once obscure vegetable is making its presence known—and a happy thing, too.

I had not even heard of cardoons—or *cardi* or *cardoni* in Italian—until I read that it was a popular dish at Harry's Bar in Venice. Cardoons are one of Nature's schizophrenic vegetables, if you will. At first glance you would think they are oversized grayish-green celery stalks. Appearances aside, they taste more like artichokes. Cardoons are also one of those mysterious vegetables that make one ponder, "Who on earth took the time to figure out how to eat them, let alone cultivate them?" Particularly because they require so much trimming and cooking before they are the least bit edible. When cooked long enough, though, the cardoon loses most of its bitterness and possesses a unique flavor all unto itself. You may find cardoons in an Italian market or specialty grocery store, but they are a rare catch. I was fortunate enough to find the plants at a farm one year. This soup may not be for everyone, and you may agree with Voltaire, who said with regard to trying something new and different, "Once a philosopher, twice a pervert." I'll take the perversion here.

As a historical tidbit, the original owner of Harry's Bar in Venice was not Harry, but Giuseppe Cipriani. The story goes that while tending bar at the Europa-Brittania Hotel, a down-on-his-luck American patron, Harry Pickering, had asked bartender Cipriani for a small loan to pay his hotel bill. Not having heard from him for two years, Cipriani assumed the debt to be lost. But Harry did return with the loan—and enough extra for Cipriani to open a watering hole and restaurant of his own: Harry's Bar. During the war, the Fascists demanded Cipriani put up a sign barring Jews. When they returned and did not find it, he took them to the kitchen, where the tiny sign hung on a back wall. They tore up the bar, and for the duration of the war it became a mess hall for German soldiers. The restaurant has since been restored to its former glory under the management of Giuseppe's son, Arrigo: Harry.

3 pounds of cardoons
A large bowl of water "acidulated" with the juice of 1 lemon
1 tablespoon extra-virgin olive oil
3 tablespoons unsalted butter
1 cup chopped leek (white and pale green parts)
2 quarts chicken stock (or the equivalent from concentrate)
Coarse or kosher salt and freshly ground pepper to taste
½ teaspoon freshly squeezed lemon juice
Garlic croutons (recipe follows)
Freshly grated Parmigiano for serving

1. Clean and trim the cardoons, outer stalks, discarding the tougher leaves. String the thick ribs with a vegetable peeler until uniform. Cut them in quarters and put them in the bowl of lemon water for 15 minutes.

2. Meanwhile, bring a large pot of water to a boil. Drain the cardoons, cut them into small pieces, and add them to the boiling water. Boil them for at least 15 minutes or longer, depending on their bitterness. Drain.

3. Heat the oil and butter in a soup pot over medium heat, and sauté the leek until it begins to wilt, about 4 minutes. Add the cooked cardoons, stirring briefly to coat them, and add the stock. Let the stock come to a boil, and reduce heat to low. Simmer for 45 minutes.

4. Let the soup cool slightly and pass it through a food mill. If you have an immersion blender, blend the soup until smooth, discarding any strings that attach to the blade. Heat the puréed soup and add the salt, pepper, and lemon juice. After a few minutes, taste for seasoning. Serve the soup with garlic croutons and grated cheese.

- -

Garlic Croutons

Although you can make croutons the conventional way in the oven, here is an easy stovetop version.

> 3 tablespoons extra-virgin olive oil
> 2 small cloves of garlic, gently smashed but intact
> ½ loaf day-old country-style bread cut into ¼-inch cubes
> (about 2 cups)
> ¼ teaspoon coarse or kosher salt

Heat a large skillet over high heat and add the olive oil, swirling to coat the bottom of the pan. Add the garlic and cook until it sizzles, about 50 seconds. Add the bread and cook, stirring, until golden brown, about 2 minutes. Discard the garlic. Sprinkle the croutons with the salt.

- -

Bread and Cheese Soup (Zuppa di Fontina)

SERVES 6

I have an old friend who loved onion soup, but as the saying goes, it did not love him. After making it for him several years ago, I regretfully say that in close company I found out why. Looking for a savory, but not viscerally debilitating, alternative, I found a very short recipe for bread soup in Ada Boni's *Italian Regional Cooking*. I have in turn married it to the onion soup, *senza le cipolle* (without the onions). Of course, the bread remains. Toasted or untoasted, the bread has always been an integral part of *zuppa*, giving it its pronounced texture. *Zuppa*, derived from the verb *inzuppare*, "to soak" or "to dunk," opened itself up to both savory and sweet dishes. Although the names may appear similar, *Zuppa di Cipolle alla Francese* is a world apart from *Zuppa Inglese*. The former is basically French onion soup, while the latter is a sponge cake or Lady Fingers dipped in liqueur.

An authentic, and truly rustic version, is *Zuppa alla Pavase*. Eggs are cracked over slices of bread in individual soup plates and topped with Parmigiano. Hot broth is poured over the eggs, thereby poaching them. According to John Mariani in his *The Dictionary of Italian Food and Drink*, the dish was said to have been created by a peasant to "restore the strength and spirits" of King Francis I after he lost the battle of Pavia in 1525. It must have worked, seeing that the king lived another twenty-two years.

12 1-inch-thick slices of country-style bread to make crostini
Extra-virgin olive oil for brushing
Salt and freshly ground pepper to taste
8 cups beef (or chicken) stock

2 tablespoons butter, softened to room temperature

½ pound Fontina, shredded, mixed with 1 cup freshly grated
  Parmigiano

Additional Parmigiano for serving

1. Preheat the oven to 350 degrees. Make the crostini. Brush both sides of the bread slices with oil and season with salt and pepper to taste. Arrange on one or two large baking sheets. Bake until golden brown, about 20 minutes, turning the bread over halfway through. Set the crostini aside.

2. Raise the oven temperature to 400 degrees. Meanwhile, bring the stock to a boil. Lower the heat and let it simmer until needed.

3. Butter the sides and bottom of an earthenware casserole dish or Dutch oven. Put alternate layers of the crostini and cheese into the bowl. Slowly pour the hot stock around the sides of the crostini so as not to soak the top layer of cheese. Bake for about 20 minutes or until the cheese has melted and is golden brown.

4. Apportion the soup and bread into shallow bowls and pass the additional Parmigiano.

You Say Tomato, I Say Thank You!

This is not so much a recipe as it is an excuse to rant about the misuse of the tomato. Barring the bath of dressing, our family salad (or *soup de salade*) generally consisted of, at the very least, tomatoes and iceberg lettuce. Oftentimes it was just the lettuce and tomato at the very most that floated in the briny drink. But the marriage of lettuce and fresh summer tomatoes, except in a sandwich, can be a remarkable mistake. When mid- to late summer is upon us, and glorious, full, ripe tomatoes are in abundance, it is criminal to defile the large, luscious fruit with leaves of any sort larger than basil. Use cherry or grape tomatoes instead. The best summer tomato salads exude their wonder from their simplicity. Thinly sliced red onion, olives, garlic, herbs, freshly ground pepper, chunks of day-old crusty bread, and, of course, good olive oil are all worthy complements. Also, do not salt the tomato slices until you are ready to serve them, as salt will draw out the juices, giving you a mealy, mushy tomato. The exception here is the *panzanella*, which needs the salt to aid in the marinating.

Naturally, there is also the unparalleled *Insalata Caprese* (salad of Capri), which is a requisite summertime dish. Composed to simulate the Italian flag of red, white, and green, the basic *Caprese* is just a mix of tomatoes, basil, and fresh mozzarella, with a dribble of fruity olive oil. Variations on the simple *Caprese* have included minced garlic, parsley, lemon juice, balsamic vinegar, sometimes served on crostini or slices of country-style bread. I think you get the idea. For larger gatherings, where "finger foods" are served, thread the basil, mozzarella chunks, and large grape tomatoes onto wooden skewers. My garden is also rife with cucumbers, and since there is always some leftover Italian or French bread, a *panzanella* is a seasonal staple. The following is my take on this earthy dish.

Panzanella

SERVES 4

3 cups ripe tomatoes, cut into 1-inch chunks

2 cups day-old crusty Italian or French bread, cut into 1-inch
chunks

1 small cucumber, peeled, seeded, and cut into large chunks (1 cup)

½ cup coarsely chopped red or Vidalia onion

1 cup torn fresh basil leaves

½ cup fruity olive oil

Dash of crushed red pepper (optional)

Coarse or kosher salt and freshly ground pepper to taste

Mix everything together and let marinate, covered loosely with plastic wrap, at room temperature. Do not refrigerate! The salad should marinate for at least 30 minutes, but it can stand for up to several hours. Toss lightly just before serving.

Caesar Salad My Way

SERVES 4 TO 6

As can be said for any great modern dish—or cocktail for that matter—many people lay claim to its invention. The *Caesar Salad* is generally attributed to the Italian restaurateur Caesar Cardini, unless you want to believe any number of his staff who also take credit. At the time of its creation, Cardini was living in San Diego but working in Tijuana. If this seems like a curious arrangement, it was because the year was 1924, and the United States was in the throes of one of its greatest follies, the Great Experiment: Prohibition. You don't have to believe me, but at that time booze was a bigger business than salads. According to Cardini's daughter, Rosa, he whipped up the dish on the Fourth of July of that year when a rush on the restaurant depleted the kitchen's supplies. As the story goes, Cardini made do with what he had, all the while entertaining his clientele by tossing the salad personally for his guests.

This theatrical touch was eventually taken over by many American chefs, and it sometimes was the sole reason for ordering the salad. The recipe also went through so many variations that on some menus you might find that the salad included mustard, avocado, tomato, bacon bits, and *even* anchovies. One chef, Nicola Paone, was fairly true to the recipe, but he went a step further with his theatrics by composing a song to accompany and elucidate the tableside prep. Molly O'Neill includes it in her *New York Cookbook*.

But wait. Even anchovies, you ask? Isn't that why so many people pass on this venerable salad? In reality, Cardini was apparently opposed to using anchovies in his version. The faint taste of anchovies from the Worcestershire sauce was sufficient for him. Cardini's brother, Alex, however, created a variation called the Aviator Salad and did include anchovies. The other significant, but little known difference is that key limes were used in the original recipe, not lemons. The change was not due to shifting taste, but to a problem in translation. When the salad was created in Mexico, the word for "lime" in Latin American Spanish was *limón*. If you look at early cocktail books, translations for the daiquiri wrongly called for lemons. I was personally confronted with this dilemma in Buenos Aires, where limes are a scarcity, despite their immense popularity just across the border in Brazil. When I asked a fruit vendor for *limas*, I was greeted with a curious look and asked what that was. "*Limón verde?*" I inquired. Aware that he had no idea of what I was talking about, I replied that it was something between a lemon and a gin and tonic.

Another difference is that Cardini originally called for whole lettuce leaves. This made complete sense for someone tossing a salad at a table. It was much easier to leave the leaves whole rather than go through an extra step of chopping or tearing. While I do see Cardini's point about the anchovies, I like their saltiness. My compromise is a dash of Thai fish sauce. I also prefer to shake the dressing in a jar to emulsify it slightly. I use raw organic free-range eggs, but if you are uncertain about your eggs, you can "coddle" them by very briefly immersing them in their shells in boiling water.

¼ teaspoon each coarse or kosher salt and freshly ground pepper, or more to taste

2 tablespoons good quality white wine vinegar (preferably aged Italian)

2 tablespoons freshly squeezed lime juice

1 large crushed and minced garlic clove

1 teaspoon Dijon mustard

1 teaspoon Worcestershire sauce

1 tablespoon Vietnamese or Thai fish sauce

2 egg yolks

½ cup extra-virgin olive oil

3 romaine lettuce hearts, chopped widthwise into 1-inch ribbons, or leaves left whole

½ cup freshly grated Parmigiano

1 cup croutons (page 79)

1. Mix all of the ingredients up to the lettuce in a jar and set aside. You may refrigerate the dressing briefly.

2. Place the romaine lettuce on a large platter and toss with the Parmigiano. Top with the croutons. Shake the jar of dressing and toss it with the salad. Serve immediately, passing extra pepper and cheese if desired.

Hearts of Romaine Lettuce with Honey and Truffle Oil Dressing and Prosciutto di Parma

SERVES 4

The iconic iceberg lettuce of my childhood is making a comeback, as are meatballs and other "comfort food." The iceberg wedge with blue cheese can be found on menus where once it would be thought of as a joke on the part of the chef. It is ironic that we never ate romaine lettuce in our home—nor knew what it was—but that iceberg should dominate over its sophisticated cousin. The mum and dad would be pleased by this retro dish.

Romaine lettuce, being firmer than other types of lettuce, lends itself to denser dressings and the addition of meats like prosciutto. Hearts of romaine usually come three to a package. Being uniform, romaine also takes nicely to quick and easy slicing. I use truffle oil here, which immediately raises the ire of many chefs. Most truffle oils are not made from actual truffles. Commercial truffle oils are concocted in the laboratory by mixing olive oil with one or more compounds like 2,4-dithiapentane (the most prominent of the hundreds of aromatic molecules that give real truffles their zing). The finest quality truffle oil is made with top-quality olive oil that has been infused with either white or black truffles. How can you tell it apart from the completely synthetic oil? Look at the price tag.

> 2 to 3 romaine lettuce hearts, cored and cut into bite-size pieces
> 2 tablespoons white truffle oil

1½ tablespoons extra-virgin olive oil

1 tablespoon white balsamic vinegar or very good white vinegar

1 tablespoon freshly squeezed lemon juice

1 teaspoon honey

Coarse or kosher salt and freshly ground pepper to taste

¼ pound prosciutto *di Parma*, thinly sliced

1 teaspoon chopped chives

Place the lettuce on a wide platter. In a small bowl, whisk together the while truffle oil, olive oil, white balsamic vinegar, lemon juice, honey, and salt and pepper. Dress the salad, top with prosciutto, and sprinkle on the chives. Serve immediately.

Grilled Romaine Lettuce with Parmigiano

SERVES 4

M y father fancied himself as the great grill man, but the hallowed Weber saw only the typical array of steak, franks, and the occasional burger. He never grilled chicken or—goodness no—fish. I am a sucker for hot dogs. But that is when somebody else makes them, since I never give in to that temptation at home (sausages are another matter). I wonder what my father would have thought of grilling vegetables, and particularly lettuce. I asked the Magic 8 Ball I still have from my youth, but the answer was "Reply hazy. Call again later."

This is a dish that straddles the demarcation of our "Salads and Sides." Romaine, being a heartier vegetable than other lettuces, but not as firm as cabbage, may be served in a salad or as an accompaniment to a main dish. Since it takes such a short time to cook, it is ideal for searing quickly on a hot grill and serving with a steak or other meats that need to rest for a few minutes. Other leafy greens that can be prepared this way are chicory and especially radicchio, sometimes known as Italian chicory. The latter, a perennial that usually has white-veined red leaves, can have something of a bitter and spicy taste when eaten raw but mellows nicely when it is grilled or roasted. For a nice touch, grill both romaine and radicchio, coarsely chop them, and serve with the following dressing.

2 tablespoons freshly squeezed lemon juice

1 tablespoon good balsamic vinegar

2 tablespoons extra-virgin olive oil

2 anchovy fillets, chopped, or a splash of Thai fish sauce (optional)

Coarse or kosher salt

2 heads romaine lettuce, trimmed and halved lengthwise

Freshly ground black pepper

Shaved Parmigiano

1. Preheat the grill to medium.

2. To make the dressing, blend lemon juice, balsamic vinegar, half the olive oil, and anchovy or fish sauce if you are using it.

3. In a large bowl, toss the 4 romaine halves in remaining olive oil and season them with salt. Arrange them in a single layer on the grill and cook for 3 minutes. Turn and cook on the other side for 3 additional minutes; the romaine should feel slightly warm and tender. Transfer the halves to a large platter. Spoon a little dressing on each and top with pepper and Parmigiano. Serve immediately.

Sautéed Tuscan Kale with Toasted Pine Nuts

SERVES 4

Bumper stickers are everywhere. In Kansas you may see "Save a cow! Eat a vegetarian." Or "I ♥ spelunking" in Tennessee. Here in my part of Western Massachusetts, one is more likely to encounter "Be a local hero," for organic farmers, or "Save Tibet," and more recently, "Eat more Kale." Seriously. Even if we had seen kale in the nearby A&P while I was growing up, it would probably have been held in no higher esteem than lawn clippings. I first took an interest in greens, like kale and chard, when Valdina brought me to Bongiorno's, a family-owned supermarket in Stamford, Connecticut. Just off of I-95, it was a godsend to the melting pot of Italian, Asian, Cuban, Puerto Rican, and black families living in the vicinity, and it catered to all of those tastes. After more than fifty years the supermarket closed in 2004 and was reopened as a Stop & Shop. At least the residents seeking diverse foodstuffs were finally gratified when a Fairway opened nearby.

Dinosaur kale, or lacinato kale as it is also known in the States, has been used for centuries in Italian cuisine, especially that of Tuscany. As popular as kale has been in Italy, you will not find it in many Italian cookbooks. Kale was denigrated as peasant food. Greens were a means of subsistence for many poor families, but they learned how to make do with little and turn what little they had into something tasty. Thanks to the interest in culinary traditions that followed the wave of nouvelle cuisine, along with the discovery of kale's nutritional value, kale has enjoyed a renaissance. Tuscan kale is also known as Tuscan cabbage, Italian kale, cavolo nero, black kale, flat back cabbage, palm tree kale, and black Tuscan palm. But I will stop there.

1½ pounds Tuscan or dinosaur (lacinato) kale (2 to 3 bunches),
     stems and ribs removed
3 tablespoons pine nuts
2 tablespoons olive oil
1½ teaspoons finely chopped garlic
½ teaspoon crushed red pepper
1 tablespoon balsamic vinegar
Coarse or kosher salt and freshly ground pepper to taste

1. Wash the kale thoroughly, but do not dry it completely. Working in batches, roll the leaves like a cigar and cut into 1-inch ribbons.

2. In a small saucepan, toast the pine nuts over medium heat. Shake the pan until the pine nuts begin to brown, about 4 minutes, and set aside.

3. Heat the oil over medium heat. Add garlic and crushed red pepper and sauté until the garlic begins to color but not brown. Add the kale and reduce the heat to low. Cover, stirring the kale occasionally, and cook until tender, 6 to 10 minutes.

4. Remove the lid and turn the heat to high, just long enough to cook off some of the liquid. Stir in the vinegar and cook for another 30 seconds. Transfer to a large bowl and top with the pine nuts. Stir in salt and pepper and serve immediately.

Grilled Sausage and Pepper and Penne Salad

SERVES 6

Pasta salads can be odious things. As an Italian American boy I found it curious that my mother would buy different kinds of pasta salads from the German deli around the corner. I instinctively winced at the sight of elbow macaroni, or worse, the overcooked shards of broken spaghetti doused with red sauce. Pasta salads, though, have become the requisite staple of potluck picnics, usually a mix of *fusilli*, vegetables, and last-minute desperation. If it hasn't already, the time may come, as it comes inevitably to all with children, when you will be "volunteered" to make a dish for a school picnic. Sooner, rather than later, that assigned dish will be a pasta salad. Do not despair. This is a dish that even you will want to eat. Unquestionably a New World entry, I won't apologize for it since it is the felicitous remedy to a necessary evil.

FOR THE GRILLED SAUSAGE AND PEPPERS:
1 medium red onion cut in half lengthwise, ends cut off, and then thinly sliced lengthwise
2 each large green and red bell peppers, cored, seeded, and cut in half lengthwise and then sliced lengthwise
¼ cup pure olive oil
6 hot (or if you prefer, sweet) Italian sausages

FOR THE PASTA:
1 pound *penne rigate* or *ziti*
6 tablespoons extra-virgin olive oil, plus more for tossing
3 tablespoons freshly squeezed lemon juice

1½ teaspoons finely grated lemon zest
1 large shallot, thinly sliced and separated into rings
Coarse or kosher salt and freshly ground black pepper to taste
1 cup halved cherry or grape tomatoes
¼ pound smoked fresh mozzarella, cut into thin strips
A handful of fresh basil leaves, torn into ½-inch pieces

1. Prepare a medium-hot fire of natural hardwood charcoal in your grill with a cover, or preheat a gas grill to medium-high.

2. Mix the onion, peppers, and olive oil in a grill basket, or on a foil-lined baking sheet. Top with the sausages. Do not pierce them! Stir in the vegetables until they are tender, about 10 minutes. Remove the vegetables from the heat and transfer to a bowl.

3. Place the sausages on the grate and grill, turning them occasionally until they are browned. When cool, slice and add them to the vegetables. This can be made ahead of time and refrigerated.

4. Bring 4 quarts of water to a boil. Salt the water, add the pasta, and cook it until al dente. Drain the pasta, reserving ¼ cup of the cooking water. Transfer the pasta to a large bowl and toss with a dash of the extra-virgin olive oil. Allow the pasta to cool.

5. Meanwhile, in a small bowl, stir the lemon juice with the lemon zest and shallot. Stir in the 3 tablespoons of extra-virgin olive oil and the reserved pasta cooking water. Stir and add salt and pepper.

6. Add the dressing to the pasta and toss well. Add the sausage, pepper, and onions, and then the tomatoes and mozzarella and toss again. Sprinkle the basil over the salad and season with salt and pepper to taste. Keep your cool.

Slow Oven-Roasted Tomatoes

MAKES APPROXIMATELY 6 TO 10 SERVINGS

When summer was gone, so were the good tomatoes my family and neighbors grew. It was back to the sordid orbs of supermarket fare. I think we might agree that there is little on the planet, or perhaps the universe, that compares to a fresh tomato. The sagacious Garrison Keillor would say fresh corn, but he would be wrong in my opinion. You may never grow bored of eating fresh tomatoes by themselves or in a *Caprese* salad, but from time to time over the summer you may have a surplus of tomatoes that is at risk of overripening. My kitchen abounds with them, and they line my windowsills, reminding me of the cult film *Attack of the Killer Tomatoes*. One solution to avoid any confrontation of that sort is slow-roasting them. Once they are done, their uses are limitless. From bruschetta to pasta, they can be used in any way you might otherwise prepare a fresh or cooked tomato. This is also a way that you can revive the lackluster off-season tomatoes.

2 pounds small, thick-walled or plum tomatoes, cored, seeded, and quartered

1 tablespoon thinly sliced garlic cloves

1 tablespoon fresh thyme leaves

1 teaspoon dried oregano

Coarse or kosher salt and freshly ground pepper to taste

¼ cup extra-virgin olive oil

½ cup fresh basil, torn into little pieces or julienned

1. Preheat oven to 250 degrees.

2. Spread the tomatoes hollow side up on a baking sheet lined with parchment paper or foil. Place a slice of garlic on each tomato and sprinkle with the thyme, oregano, and salt and pepper. Drizzle the olive oil over the tomatoes.

3. Roast in the oven for 1 to 2 hours, or until the tomatoes begin to shrivel to about half their size. Let cool before serving. Sprinkle the tomatoes with the fresh basil.

4. If you are not serving the tomatoes immediately, place them in a container with their juice. Place a piece of plastic wrap over them to seal them. Cover and refrigerate.

Baked Stuffed Tomatoes with Lamb Ragù

SERVES 6

W hen I was teaching art history at the Fashion Institute of Technology in New York City (when the world was young), I had a contingent of Greek students who swore that I was of Greek descent. They regaled me with music and books so that I could restore my proper heritage. They also knew that lamb was one of my favorite dishes, and one day one of the students brought me *Yemistes Domates me Rizi*—baked tomatoes with lamb. I did not dare tell them that I would attempt to translate this recipe into my own true Italian heritage. Using my meat *ragù* I have done my best to purloin the Greek rudiments of the dish and literally recast it in an Italian mold. The best tomatoes to bake with are a thick-walled variety. I prefer Brandywine, but Beefsteak tomatoes are excellent as well. This mixture is also perfect for stuffed peppers.

⅓ cup Arborio rice (or other short-grain white rice)

6 large, ripe tomatoes

Coarse or kosher salt and freshly ground pepper to taste

½ recipe for Lamb Ragù (page 137)

Toasted pine nuts (page 91)

½ cup freshly grated Pecorino Romano

2 tablespoons extra-virgin olive oil, plus more for drizzling

A handful of fresh basil leaves, torn into ½-inch pieces

1. Preheat the oven to 375 degrees. **2.** Precook the rice by boiling it in salted water until it is three-fourths of the way done, about 8 minutes, and let cool slightly.

3. Meanwhile, cut a ½-inch-thick slice off the top of each tomato. Trim and reserve the tomato tops and set aside. Scoop out the seeds and discard. Scoop out the pulp as well and chop along with the reserved tops. Add this and any juice from the tomatoes to a medium-size bowl with the salt and pepper. Then add the rice, meat sauce, and pine nuts. Blend in half the cheese.

4. Oil the bottom of an 8 x 8-inch baking dish with the olive oil. Fill the tomatoes with the lamb mixture, sprinkle the rest of the cheese on top, and drizzle with olive oil. Bake for about 30 minutes or until the tomatoes are wrinkled and soft and the rice is tender. Sprinkle on the basil and serve warm or at room temperature.

Balsamic Roasted Brussels Sprouts

SERVES 4

John Waters referred to Brussels sprouts as "little green balls from hell." I doubt if my mother has ever heard of Mr. Waters, let alone (heaven help us) seen any of his films. Nor do I know if she concurred with his opinion, but when I was a tyke, the only curiosity raised in me about the Brussels sprouts I saw in the store was why they were packaged in cups. This recipe is so simple that there are few variations out there. Still, my family is so loopy over the Brussels sprouts that I was induced to include them here. We especially like them in the autumn when you can buy them still on the stalk at the local farm stands.

> 2 to 3 cups Brussels sprouts, sliced in half, or quartered if very large
>
> 3 tablespoons extra-virgin olive oil
>
> Coarse or kosher salt and freshly ground pepper to taste
>
> 2 tablespoons balsamic vinegar

1. Preheat oven to 400 degrees.

2. Toss the Brussels sprouts with the oil and salt and pepper, and spread them out cut side down in a single layer on a baking sheet.

3. Bake for 30 minutes, turning once. The sprouts are done when they are browned and some of the outer leaves are charred. Transfer to a bowl and toss them with the balsamic vinegar. Serve immediately.

Caponatina

SERVES 6 AS AN APPETIZER

I don't know if my father was in a state of rebellion after his retirement, but being stuck around the house compelled him to embark upon several endeavors he had previously ignored entirely. One was driving. He hadn't driven since he was in the army. At sixty-six he surprised everyone as he drove up to the house in a used Toyota Corolla. I suppose that he just needed something to occupy himself besides monitoring all of the activity on the block. He was even nicknamed the Mayor of Coolidge Avenue. The other enterprise he took to was even more bizarre: He began cooking on the stove, and not just at the grill! I suppose that he just needed to have something good to eat in the house besides pretzels and fruit. Living between Massachusetts and Argentina, I had little opportunity to sample his experiments, but he would save me a jar of his homemade *caponata*. He endearingly referred to it in the southern Italian dialect as *caponatina*. This is my re-creation.

> 2 eggplants, about 1 pound each, unpeeled, cut into ½-inch cubes
> Coarse or kosher salt to "sweat" the eggplant
> 5 tablespoons olive oil
> 1 celery heart, cut into ½-inch pieces
> 1 medium onion, cubed (about ¾ cup)
> 1½ teaspoons chopped garlic
> 1 14.5-ounce can diced tomatoes (I like Muir Glen Fire Roasted tomatoes for this)
> 3 tablespoons red wine vinegar
> 2 tablespoons drained capers
> Coarse or kosher salt and freshly ground pepper to taste
> ⅓ cup chopped fresh basil

1. Sprinkle the eggplants with salt and let them stand in a colander for about an hour to "sweat" them of their bitter juices. Dry them well.

2. Heat the oil in a large sauté pan over medium-high heat until rippling and fry the eggplant, in batches if necessary, until browned. Drain them on paper towels. Follow this procedure for the celery.

3. Adding more oil if needed, lower heat to medium and briefly sauté the onion and garlic until soft, about 4 minutes. Stir in the diced tomatoes with their juice, the vinegar, and the capers. Cook for about 10 minutes.

4. Add the eggplant and celery to the tomatoes. Lower the heat and simmer, stirring occasionally, for about 10 minutes more until the *cap-*

onatina just begins to thicken. Season with salt and pepper. Mix in the fresh basil. Transfer *the caponatina* to a serving bowl, cool, and refrigerate until ready. Serve cold or at room temperature as a dip or on crusty bread.

Ciambotta with Fried Capers

SERVES 4 AS A MAIN COURSE OR 6 AS AN APPETIZER

Sometimes, when staying with Nanny on Fridays while my mother had her hair done, I would mix my TV dinner and sandwiches all together on my plate. She would shake her head and say I was making—as I understood it—*chambot*. It was only recently that I learned that this nonsense word is actually derived from a southern Italian summer vegetable stew, *ciambotta*. I have since left Swanson's chopped sirloin and mashed potato TV dinner portions tucked into a grilled cheese English muffin to distant (far distant) memory. This recipe is hardly reminiscent of that fiasco. Rather, it is an excellent way to take full advantage of the highpoint of summer's vegetable bounty. The best choices for tomatoes here are Brandywines, Big Boys, or other large, meaty tomatoes. I also like smaller, Asian fingerling eggplants for this. They are firmer and give off less moisture.

According to Carlo Middione, in *The Food of Southern Italy*, *ciambotta* is always served hot. Personally, I think you could serve it at room temperature and find it no less satisfying. The recipe that follows is a variation on one I found on the delightful Web site of author/cook Erica De Mane (ericademane.com).

2 pounds ripe but firm fresh tomatoes

2 tablespoons extra-virgin olive oil, plus more for drizzling and frying

½ cup chopped young spring onions or ramps

½ cup chopped tender celery stalks, reserving the leaves for
   garnishing

1 cup seeded and finely diced red or yellow bell pepper

1 tablespoon seeded and finely chopped hot pepper

1 tablespoon thinly sliced garlic cloves

½ pound new potatoes, peeled and cut into small cubes

½ pound eggplant, unpeeled, cut into small cubes

½ pound zucchini or summer squash (or both mixed), cut into
   small cubes

Coarse or kosher salt and freshly ground pepper to taste

½ cup capers, drained and patted dry

¼ cup dry white wine

A handful of basil leaves, lightly torn

1. Seed and coarsely chop the tomatoes and set them in a colander over a bowl. Lightly salt them and let them drain for about half an hour, reserving the liquid.

2. Heat the 2 tablespoons of oil in a large skillet over medium-high heat. Add the onions, celery, bell pepper, and the hot pepper, and sauté for about 4 minutes. Add the garlic and the potatoes and sauté another minute. Add the eggplant and zucchini with the salt and pepper and continue cooking for another 4 minutes or so to incorporate all the ingredients.

3. Meanwhile, over medium-high heat, Pour in just enough olive oil to cover the bottom of a small skillet. When the oil is hot, add the capers and fry them until they crisp. Drain on paper towels and set aside. Serve hot.

4. Raise heat slightly under the vegetables and pour in the wine, allowing it to come to a boil. Lower heat to medium and add the tomatoes. Simmer for about 8 minutes or until all the vegetables begin to soften, adding the reserved tomato water if necessary. The dish should have the consistency of a stew (think ratatouille). Stir and further season to taste. Scatter the capers over the vegetables and drizzle on olive oil to taste. Add the basil and the celery leaves. You can serve this immediately or let it cool and serve it as you would *caponata* with good crusty bread.

Slow-Roasted Party Olives

SERVES MANY

W hen my family decided to have a real bang-up celebration—say, for New Year's Eve—it wasn't just the simple bag of Wise potato chips, or any other number of packaged Planter's peanuts, Bachman pretzels, or Dipsy Doodles unceremoniously plopped into a bowl. No, sir. Out came the Ritz crackers and Velveeta (that miraculous concoction Easy Cheese in the aerosol can came later, and it was all one could do to stop me from sucking it right out of the nozzle). Otherwise it was a bowl of onion dip freshly made from instant Lipton Soup mix and sour cream. If it was really a special occasion, there were pigs in a blanket. Inevitably, there were also canned Lindsay olives. Those olives I knew growing up were pitted black things that you slipped on your fingers, waved around a bit, and then methodically ate. Upon reflection, they faintly remind me of what the Tin Man in the *Wizard of Oz* was made of. I relished them, so to speak, without knowing that there was something else out there: olives—real olives.

Nearly every Western and Near Eastern country routinely serves olives as a beloved snack— except the United States and parts of Canada. I am certain that many North Americans outside of urban areas have never tasted anything save for what escaped from a can or a jar. During my first years at the Blue Heron, we gave all of our clientele a small bowl of roasted olives. Some people begged for more. Others, having only been familiar with the kind that were adulterated with ferrous gluconate (an iron derivative), eyed them with suspicion or summarily ignored them. Those folks caused us to practically cry because when they did not touch them, we were forced to toss them into the trash. If you have never worked in a restaurant, you too might weep at the food that ends up in the dumpster.

What makes roasted olives the ideal party snack is that you can prepare them well ahead of time and quickly reheat them in a pan just before serving. You may use any number of imported whole, *unpitted* olives, but I would recommend a variety of green and black, and large and small (such as Kalamata, niçoise, Arbequina, Cerignola, Picholine, and oil-cured black olives). The following recipe is my take on how to prepare this tiny, delectable fruit.

1 pound of mixed black and green imported olives, drained

6 large garlic cloves, peeled and lightly smashed

4 tablespoons chopped, mixed fresh herbs (rosemary and oregano or thyme, for example)

½ teaspoon crushed red pepper

Julienned zest of 1 lemon

½ cup extra-virgin olive oil

¼ cup red wine vinegar

Coarse or kosher salt and freshly ground pepper to taste

1. Preheat the oven to 350 degrees.

2. In a medium bowl, combine all of the ingredients and mix well. Transfer the olive mixture to a roasting pan. Bake for 30 minutes. Serve immediately or cool and refrigerate. If you have made them ahead of time, simply reheat them in a skillet until warm.

Grilled Provolone

SERVES 4

For me, provolone was either melted on a sandwich or served with an antipasto. When I lived in Buenos Aires, however, I learned how the Argentinians took it a step further. The Italian immigrants to Argentina brought many of their traditional recipes with them. Whatever food they could not find, they grew or made. It is difficult to walk a few blocks in the center of Buenos Aires without coming upon a pasta shop selling all manner of fresh pasta, including *tortellini*, ravioli, and *gnocchi*—or as they spell it *ñoqui*. One custom is Ñoqui Day, celebrated on the last day of every month. Traditionally, money is placed under a plate of *ñoquis* in hopes of bringing prosperity in the month to come. At the same time, the Italians there have also embraced many of the cooking methods of Argentina.

One marriage of Argentina and Italy is cooking provolone on a grill (provoleta). It is a bit tricky heating cheese over a fire, but it produces an ultimately satisfying dish. If you are wary of this process, you could lightly oil a cast-iron griddle or frying pan and cook the provolone as per the directions that follow. Most Argentines serve this grilled cheese with their piquant garlic sauce, *chimichurri*, but it is just as common in Argentine Italian cuisine to serve this dish with tomato sauce. Loving all cheese, and especially provolone, the Argentines also produce a harder *grana* provolone for grating.

Olive oil for brushing the grill
2 pieces of provolone sliced 1 inch thick (about ½ pound)
2 tablespoons dried oregano
1 teaspoon crushed red pepper
Tomato sauce of your choice, heated

1. Heat a hardwood charcoal fire, or preheat a gas grill, to medium-high. Brush the grill with the olive oil to help prevent sticking.

2. Press half the oregano and crushed red pepper onto both sides of the cheese. When the grill is ready, place the cheese slices directly on the grill and cook for about 2 minutes on each side, or until the cheese is hot, slightly browned, but still holding its shape. Remove the cheese from the grill and top with the remaining oregano and pepper. Pour a large dollop of warm tomato sauce on top and serve immediately.

Frico from Friuli-Venezia Giulia

MAKES 2 LARGE PANCAKES

An old potato chip advertisement had a young boy dare Bert Lahr (aka the Cowardly Lion in the *Wizard of Oz*) to eat just one Lay's potato chip. TV ads like that made potato chips irresistible. There were always bags of potato chips in our house. My sister loved them so much, I bet her a thousand dollars she could not go ten years without eating one. Yes, that was fairly stupid on my part, but after a year, seeing her misery, I revoked the bet. Even if you can pass that test, you will most assuredly not be able to eat just one *frico*.

Originating back in the fourteenth century in Friuli-Venezia Giulia, located in the foothills of the Alps, *frico* is a cooked cheese that is not at all common in other parts of Italy. Local Montasio was, and still is in Friuli, the ideal cheese for this crispy delight, although Parmigiano has usurped it in the United States. The technique for making the small crisps in the United States is quite different from the technique used to make them in Friuli, where Montasio cheese is fried in a pan like a pancake with olive oil until hardened and crisp. The *frico* is then broken up and eaten as a snack or appetizer. It can also be shaped into a basket or small cup to hold antipasti.

Young Montasio cheese will result in a *frico* that is soft and cheesy in the middle, while aged Montasio cheese will yield a crispier *frico*. For our recipe, we will use Montasio *stagionato*, which is aged for up to two years. This is one of those recipes where you can mix in other ingredients such as black pepper, rosemary, or anything you like. *Frico* is also cooked like an omelet, where ingredients such as potatoes or seafood are sautéed, and the cheese added to them.

    1 teaspoon extra-virgin olive oil
    12 ounces aged Montasio, shredded or cut into small strips

In a nonstick frying pan, heat the oil over medium heat. Sprinkle the Montasio into the pan. When the edges start to brown, flip the *frico* and cook the other side. To shape it, keep the *frico* warm until ready to mold; it hardens quickly as it cools. To form cups, press the *frico* onto the bottom and over the sides of a mini muffin pan. Otherwise, wait till the *frico* hardens and break it into pieces.

For an interesting modern take on *frico*, slightly sauté your favorite salsa to remove any excess liquid. Add the cheese and cook as usual.

Fried Zucchini Slices

SERVES 4

Nanny was addicted to breading and frying almost anything. Eggplant and squash were at the top of the list. She even breaded and fried squash blossoms, which made me wonder if the azaleas would be next. Not accustomed to seeing squash in our home in any form, my narrow juvenile mind was suspicious. Zucchini has gotten a raw deal throughout recent history. Dr. Samuel Johnson may have been referring to the preparation of cucumbers when he said the following: "Slice it, dress it with salt, pepper, and vinegar, and throw it out as good for nothing." John Thorne gives zucchini equal truck in his *Simple Cooking*, where he appraises it as "a vegetable with the nutritious value, flavor, and texture of rained-on newspaper." One of the reasons, if not the primary reason, is that zucchini releases an overabundance of liquid when cooked in such dishes as ratatouille. One can salt zucchini and put them in a colander, as you would eggplant, but quickly frying zucchini in hot oil sears the little devils and inhibits the dispersal of their moisture. Moreover, if you have a garden, you can obviate the problem of too much moisture by picking them when they are young, and not much longer than your middle finger.

Zucchini and summer squash are now constant companions in my garden. A word of caution, though, to the novice gardener: Zucchini are the rabbits of the vegetable world. Your vegetable patch will be overrun with a fecund bounty of the blighters. I am not the only one who has been faced with this dilemma apparently, because there is a joke in these parts (and maybe your area, too) that goes like this: "Our neighborhood is so safe that the only time we lock our cars is in August, to prevent people from putting zucchini in the backseat." Here again is a reason to pick zucchini when they are young, as several small zucchini are far more serviceable to cooking than one the size of kid-sized Whiffle bat.

I may never have tasted my grandmother's fried zucchini, but I did sample the ones served at the New York Harry's bar and restaurant in the Sherry-Netherland Hotel. My memory is a bit cloudy as to how they may have made them, as Harry's martinis were seemingly made with ice formed from the water of the river Lethe (the river of forgetfulness), but I think this is a fair adaptation.

1 cup flour
1 cup dried breadcrumbs or *panko*
Coarse or kosher salt and freshly ground pepper to taste
2 eggs
½ cup extra-virgin olive oil
4 medium zucchini (no longer than 6 inches) sliced into thin rounds

1. Blend the flour, breadcrumbs, and salt and pepper on a plate. Break the eggs in a shallow bowl, beat, and set alongside.

2. Heat the oil over medium-high heat in a large sauté pan. Dip the zucchini rounds in the egg, letting the excess drip back into the bowl, and lightly press them into the flour and breadcrumb mixture on both sides. Working in batches, place the zucchini in the hot oil for about 3 minutes per side or until golden. Do not crowd them, or they will not brown properly. Drain them on paper towels and keep each batch warm in a low oven until all the zucchini are done. Use this method for frying squash blossoms as well.

Frittata with Grape Tomatoes, Mushrooms, and Prosciutto

SERVES 6

My family was not particularly keen on eggs. They were considered almost exclusively something to be eaten for breakfast. In our house, breakfast was usually cold cereal. This was a good thing. I don't want to imply that Cap'n Crunch or Trix were nutritionally sound options. They were merely palatable and aesthetic alternatives, and Red Baron had not yet come along with their breakfast pizzas, with the slogan: "There's nothing better than bacon for breakfast, unless it's a Red Baron Biscuit-Style Bacon Scrambles Pizza." Scrambled eggs, meanwhile, were minor atrocities. Lumpy and never fully whisked together, they sat in a coagulating clump on your plate, defying you to eat them. I declined. Soft-boiled eggs were so runny that you could not catch them. I don't think my mother ever even tried to master the fine art of frying an egg. She did make hard-boiled eggs, but they were severely overcooked and were rubbery with greenish-gray yolks. I think Dr. Seuss may have gotten the idea for *Green Eggs and Ham* from one of my mother's aberrations. They may have been edible, but they were abominable to look at.

My mother's eggs were so loathsome that it wasn't until I was married that I began to eat cooked eggs (although I still have issues with hard-boiled eggs). We are so fortunate to have fresh hen and duck eggs available to us all year round that the dilemma we often face is which local farm we should buy from. I don't make *frittatas* often, and when I do it is usually very late in the morning—and generally for guests who are a bit bleary-eyed from overindulging in the fruits of Bacchus the night before. I have included a particular recipe below, but my usual version is a mix of eggs and whatever I find in the fridge. If there is one dish that is a palette for your palate, it is the *frittata*.

1 tablespoon unsalted butter
¼ cup chopped onion
½ cup thinly sliced cremini mushrooms
1 cup halved grape (or cherry) tomatoes
6 eggs, beaten
1 ounce Parmigiano freshly grated, plus more for topping
½ cup julienned prosciutto
Coarse or kosher salt and freshly ground pepper to taste
1 tablespoon julienned fresh basil

1. Preheat your oven to broil.

2. Heat a 12-inch nonstick pan over medium heat and melt the butter. Add the onion and mushrooms and cook until soft, about 5 minutes. Stir in the tomatoes and cook for another 2 minutes. Set aside to cool briefly.

3. In medium-size bowl, using a fork or whisk, blend together the eggs, Parmigiano, prosciutto, and salt and pepper. Add the onion, mushroom, and tomato mixture to the eggs. Pour the egg mixture into the same pan and stir with a wooden or rubber spatula. Cook until the egg mixture has set on the bottom and the sides begin to brown, about 5 minutes.

4. Sprinkle the top evenly with the remaining Parmigiano and set under the broiler until the cheese melts and the *frittata* is golden brown, about 3 minutes. Sprinkle with the basil and serve immediately.

Frittata di Scammaro

SERVES 4 AS A PASTA OR MAIN COURSE,

6 TO 8 AS AN ANTIPASTO

If we never had a *frittata* made with eggs at home, then one made with other ingredients would have been unfathomable. Spaghetti was for the pot, not the pan. Although this dish is called a *frittata*, it is not made with eggs. But since "*frittata*" simply refers to the way it is cooked, nobody should complain. This cake of fried spaghetti is seasoned with the usual and much-beloved Neapolitan condiments of garlic, olives, anchovies, capers, hot pepper, and parsley. *Scammaro* refers to days of fasting, and this is one of the so-called lean dishes that you can have before Easter on fasting days. But why wait? It can be served as part of a main course, but Neapolitans also enjoy it as a snack. If you find the taste or texture of anchovies less than satisfying, you can always substitute a few splashes of fish sauce. Be warned, *scammaro* is addictive! Because of the saltiness of the capers and anchovies, you do not need to add any salt.

12 ounces thin spaghetti

¼ cup plus 2 tablespoons extra-virgin olive oil

2 large cloves garlic, finely chopped

½ cup pitted and coarsely chopped Gaeta, Kalamata, or other black olives

3 anchovy fillets, rinsed

2 tablespoons rinsed and coarsely chopped capers

¼ cup coarsely chopped pine nuts

¼ teaspoon (or less to taste) crushed red pepper

1 rounded tablespoon finely cut parsley

1. Bring 4 quarts of water to a boil. Salt the water, add the spaghetti, and cook until al dente. Drain well.

2. Set a 10-inch nonstick omelet pan or cast-iron skillet over medium-low heat. Add the ¼ cup oil and the garlic and cook for a minute, but before it begins to color. Stir in the olives, anchovies, capers, pine nuts, crushed red pepper, and parsley. Increase the heat very slightly and cook for 3 to 5 minutes, mashing the anchovies into the oil until they dissolve. Transfer the mixture to a large bowl. Add the spaghetti and toss well to combine all the ingredients.

3. Raise the heat under the pan to medium and add the remaining 2 tablespoons of oil. When the oil begins to ripple, pour in the spaghetti mixture, distributing it evenly and pressing it down with the back of a wooden spoon (or better yet, set another frying pan atop the pasta). Cook, continuing to press down occasionally with a wooden spoon, until the bottom and sides of the *frittata* are well browned, about 15 minutes. Slide the *frittata* onto a large dinner plate or platter, then flip it back into the pan with the uncooked side down and repeat the cooking process for another 15 minutes. As the *frittata* fries, rotate a knife or spatula around the edge to prevent it from sticking to the pan. Shake the pan occasionally so the bottom doesn't stick. When all sides have browned well, slide the *frittata* onto the large dinner plate or serving platter.

4. Serve hot, warm, or at room temperature, cut into wedges, as an antipasto, first course, or second course.

Muffuletta

SERVES 4

A list of ingredients that you would find in any Italian town would include salami, ham, mortadella, provolone, garlic, olives, and olive oil, among many other staples that have crossed the ocean with the Italian immigrants. If there is one meal that is an entire distillation of pure Italian ingredients translated into the American Italian vocabulary, it is the muffuletta.

Some might think it odd to include a dish, or more likely a vast platter, of cold cut–laden bread that is a trademark New Orleans food, but Louisiana at the beginning of the last century was home to nearly twenty thousand Italians. They may have been welcomed as workers toiling the fields and picking cotton, but they were not accepted as Americans. Despite the low opinion of these immigrants, restaurants throughout the French Quarter served up heaps of spaghetti and macaroni that was made fresh daily. The Italian Central Grocery store's original owner, Salvatore Lupo, invented it to feed the Sicilian truck farmers who sold their produce at the farmers market on Decatur Street. Central Grocery is a stomping ground for locals and a mecca for tourists.

Thanks to the publication of my *Field Guide to Cocktails*, I had the opportunity to take part in the Tales of the Cocktail event, held in New Orleans every July. NOLA is the ultimate food city where gourmets and gourmands alike want to go to die. After a night of rubbing—and bending—elbows with some of the world's best bartenders, the effects of the "bending" had a way of diminishing one's capacity to perambulate with any proficiency the following morning. The sure cure is a muffuletta from Central Grocery at the far end of Decatur Street. There have been fisticuffs over who makes the best po' boy in NOLA: Domilise's, Guy's, Mother's? Hands down, or hands full when it comes to the muffuletta, the winner is the one and only Central Grocery. Many have tried to duplicate their amazing olive salad, and I include one version below. The process is time-consuming and a little labor-intensive, but you can save yourself the trouble now that Central Grocery finally has made its alchemical mix available online (see Mail-order and Online Sources). If you have never been to NOLA, this is one of about a thousand reasons to go—posthaste.

FOR THE SANDWICH (IF I MAY BE SO BOLD TO CALL IT THAT—
   THE EARL NEVER HAD THIS IN MIND):
10-inch flat round loaf of Italian bread with sesame seeds
Olive Salad (recipe below)

4 ounces thinly sliced Genoa salami

4 ounces thinly sliced cooked ham

4 ounces thinly sliced mortadella

4 ounces thinly sliced mozzarella

4 ounces thinly sliced provolone

Cut the bread in half lengthwise. Hollow out some of the excess bread to make room for the filling. Spread the bottom layer of the bread with olive salad, including some of the oil. Layer the bread with the salami, ham, mortadella, mozzarella, and provolone. Top with more of the olive salad and replace the top half of the bread, cut the muffuletta into quarters, and pass the napkins.

Olive Salad

1 cup chopped pimento-stuffed green olives

½ cup pitted and chopped Kalamata olives

1½ teaspoons minced garlic

¼ cup roughly chopped pickled cauliflower florets

2 tablespoons drained capers

1 tablespoon chopped celery

1 tablespoon chopped carrot

½ cup drained and chopped pepperoncini

1 teaspoon dried oregano

Freshly ground black pepper to taste

¼ cup red wine vinegar

½ cup extra-virgin olive oil

In a medium bowl, combine all the ingredients. Mix everything together and transfer the mixture to a glass jar. If needed, pour in more oil to cover. Cover the jar or container and refrigerate for at least 2 days before using.

Spring Risotto with Gorgonzola, Ramps, and Cherry Tomatoes

SERVES 4

With Minute Rice as the family choice of rice, it would have taken a surfeit of hallucinogens to convince my mother to take the time to cook *risotto*. In truth, I detested Minute Rice. It did not even look like rice. The ends were coarse rather than smooth, and I wondered if all the grains of rice came from one long strand that had been broken into tiny pieces. If Arborio rice was a thing of mystery to us, ramps were the inhabitants of a distant galaxy. *Allium tricoccum*, commonly known as a ramp or wild leek, possesses a duality that is prized by lovers of garlic and onions. Ramps are an early spring vegetable that are classed as wild onions, but ramps are complemented by a pronounced garlicky aroma. Ramps are also fabulous by themselves, simply grilled with olive oil and then topped with a dribble of balsamic.

The growing period for ramps is all too short, so this dish is best made in the spring when ramps are available—if you can find them. Although they are becoming more common in the northern states, they have been prized in the South for decades. There are even ramp festivals. Indeed, the mountain folk of Appalachia have long celebrated spring with the arrival of the ramp, believing that it has great power as a tonic to ward off many of the ailments of winter. Purely as an aside, the ramp was called *chicagou* by the native tribes inhabiting the early land around (you guessed it) Chicago.

Clearly, if there is any dish that can function as your canvas, it is *risotto*. *Pancetta* is an ideal partner. It should be added at the beginning, along with onions or shallots, for example. Reconstituted porcini mushrooms should be added midway through the cooking, along with their strained soaking liquid. Vegetables like zucchini or peas may be added toward the end, allowing them merely to heat through but remain crisp-tender. Some people prefer to add red wine for color, but as important as presentation is, I maintain that in the end you do not taste with your eyes.

As for the soft cheese, in the following recipe, I prefer Gorgonzola *dolce* to regular Gorgonzola *piccante*. It is creamier and milder than its firmer counterpart. It will blend more readily into the *risotto* than will other Gorgonzolas. As for the rice, Carnaroli and Vialone Nano will cook up less sticky than Arborio, and the smaller grain Vialone will take less time. Always serve *risotto* on flat plates or shallow soup plates so that it can spread out and cool without cooking any further.

If I may pass on a little-known Italian flavor enhancer, here is another use for your Parmigiano cheese rinds. Let them simmer slowly in your stock until their essence is leached out of them. Try this as well when you are making a more delicate *risotto*, such as a *risotto alla Milanese*, a simple *risotto* with stock, wine, and saffron. The subtle complexity of your *risotto* may astound you.

¼ pound seeded and coarsely chopped cherry or
   grape tomatoes
1 cup coarsely chopped ramps
2 tablespoons extra-virgin olive oil
1 tablespoon balsamic vinegar
8 cups chicken or beef stock
2 tablespoons unsalted butter
2 cups, Carnaroli, Arborio rice, or Vialone Nano
½ cup dry white wine at room temperature
¼ pound Gorgonzola *dolce*
Coarse or kosher salt and freshly ground pepper to taste
Freshly grated Parmigiano for serving

1. Mix together the tomatoes, ¼ cup of the ramps, and 1 tablespoon of the olive oil and the vinegar.

2. Bring the chicken or beef stock to a slow, rolling bubble. Heat the butter in a 5- to 6-quart skillet or casserole over medium heat. Add ½ cup of the ramps and stir until soft, about 3 minutes. Add the rice, and using a wooden spatula, stir the rice for about 2 minutes until it starts to look chalky and you can see a white dot in the center of each grain. Add the white wine and stir. When the wine has nearly evaporated, start ladling in about ¾ cup of the stock at a time. Only add the next ladleful of stock after the previous liquid has been completely absorbed. Adjust heat as necessary to maintain a steady simmer. Keep stirring the rice from the sides to the center, folding it so that it will cook uniformly. About halfway through (4 cups of stock), add a tablespoon of the grated Parmigiano. Once 5 cups of the liquid have been absorbed, add the stock in half portions. Begin tasting the rice. If it looks like you may not have enough stock, add hot water before you run out. Do not overcook the rice. It should be tender but still a tad firm, and never mushy. The entire process should take from 15 to 20 minutes, depending on the rice you use.

3. Add the remaining ¼ cup ramps, the Gorgonzola, and salt and pepper, and blend thoroughly.

4. Spoon the *risotto* onto flat plates or very shallow soup plates. Top each with an equal amount of the tomato topping and pass the Parmigiano.

Grilled Polenta with Fontina, Asparagus, and Tomato Sauce

SERVES 4

Polenta has historically been excoriated as peasant food. I doubt if that was the reason we were never served it, since there were plenty of other victuals we were given that could have qualified as such. Still, I knew nothing of polenta until I was in my late thirties.

This yellow corn meal is served throughout Italy, and the ingredients will reflect the region just as dialects distinguish the Milanese from the Sicilians. Quality and prices vary just as much. You can pay a couple of euros for it at a fast-food chain, or you can break the bank for a plate of Beef Daube in Red Wine with Polenta at Milan's Cracco—*ragùs* to riches. Not every quick-cooking foodstuff is without merit. Polenta, our Italian take on grits, is certainly one of the better ones. Instead of stirring a pot for upwards of half an hour, a minute to 5 minutes of cooking will do for most instant polenta, particularly if you are going to grill it. I had worked with the late Michael McLaughlin on the press material for several of his books, and he introduced me to grilled polenta. This recipe is dedicated to him. And I think he would enjoy this very much with a glass of hearty, but low-tannic wine, like a Barbera.

Also, did you know that the preferred way of eating whole spears of asparagus, listed in etiquette books, is with your fingers?

1 pound thin asparagus

Polenta (recipe follows)

1 tablespoon extra-virgin olive oil

Coarse or kosher salt and freshly ground pepper to taste

2 cups Long-Simmered Summer Tomato Sauce (page 59) or your favorite sauce

½ cup coarsely shredded Fontina

1 teaspoon dried oregano

1. Trim or snap off the woody ends of the asparagus, and peel the lower green portion if the asparagus is too thick. Cook in salted water or steam until crisp-tender. Drain and refresh the spears in cold water. Cut them into 4-inch pieces.

2. Prepare a medium-hot fire of natural hardwood charcoal in your grill with a cover, or preheat a gas grill to medium-high.

3. Carefully remove the polenta from its pan and cut into 4-inch squares. Brush the squares with the olive oil and sprinkle on the salt and pepper.

4. When the grill is ready, place the squares of polenta on the grate and cook for about 5 minutes per side, or until you see grill marks on the polenta. Don't turn them too quickly, as they need time to develop a char and will otherwise fall apart.

5. In a baking pan just large enough to accommodate the polenta, spread the tomato sauce evenly across the bottom. Add the polenta squares. Place the asparagus on the squares and top with the cheese and the oregano.

6. Place the pan back on the grill and cover. Cook until the cheese begins to brown, about 10 minutes.

Polenta

Instant polenta for 4
Water or chicken broth
Coarse or kosher salt (if using water) and freshly ground
     pepper
¾ cup freshly grated Parmigiano
Olive oil for coating the pan

Cook the polenta in water or broth according to directions on the package, adding the Parmigiano cheese as soon as the polenta has blended together. When the polenta is done, spoon it into an 8-inch pan that has been coated with the oil. Using a spatula, smooth the top of the polenta until it is even. Let the polenta come to room temperature. Cover with plastic wrap and refrigerate overnight.

Stuffed and Rolled Peppers, Lipari Style

SERVES 4 AS A SIDE DISH

When my mother was not in the room, my father would occasionally look up from a plate of what he may have indecorously described to me as "who-did-it-and-ran," and ask the ceiling why we couldn't have escarole soup or stuffed peppers the way his mother had made them. His mother died two months before I was born, so I never had the opportunity to meet her, let alone taste her southern Italian food. His family was from Lipari, the largest of the Aeolian Islands off the north coast of Sicily. I was told that they were the first family on the island to have an indoor working toilet. I suppose it's always good to be the first at something. I am sad to say, though, that I never had the chance of making this recipe for him.

BELL PEPPER

The cheese used here is a dry version of ricotta: *ricotta salata*. This firm, slightly sharp cheese is usually made from the whey that is a by-product of the Pecorino Romano cheesemaking process. The curds are put in a basket mold and pressed. Salt is added to extract moisture and make the curds compact enough to produce a uniform, dry, spongy texture. The salt gives the cheese its sharp taste. *Ricotta* is an Italian word meaning "recooked," while *salata* means "salted." *Ricotta salata* has a firm texture that makes it a favorite for tossing, grating, slicing, and crumbling.

2 large yellow peppers

2 large red peppers

2 tablespoons extra-virgin olive oil, plus more for drizzling

½ pound cremini mushrooms, cleaned and coarsely chopped

Coarse or kosher salt and freshly ground black pepper

¼ pound *ricotta salata*, coarsely grated

1 ounce dried porcini mushrooms, soaked in hot water, drained, carefully washed and finely chopped

2 tablespoons chopped fresh parsley

2 tablespoons toasted and coarsely chopped pine nuts (page 91)

4 tablespoons freshly grated Pecorino Romano

1. Preheat oven to 350 degrees. Place the peppers in a shallow baking pan and roast them for from 15 to 20 minutes until they begin to blister. Remove them to a brown paper bag and allow them to cool. Once they have cooled, peel off the skin, discard the seeds, and cut the peppers in half lengthwise. Set the peppers cut-side down on a cutting board or other smooth surface.

2. Heat the oil in a large sauté pan over medium-high heat and cook all the mushrooms, turning them often, until lightly browned, about 10 minutes. Season them with salt and pepper and set aside. In another bowl, mix together the *ricotta salata*, porcini mushrooms, parsley, and pine nuts. Add the cremini mushrooms, mix well, and adjust seasonings.

3. Set your oven to broil. Divide the mushroom mixture among the 8 pepper halves. Roll each pepper, leaving the seam side down, and place on a lightly greased baking pan. Sprinkle on the grated cheese, drizzle lightly with olive oil, and broil until the cheese begins to take on color, about 5 minutes.

A Word About Potatoes

Another happy accident occurred one day when my mother did not want to dirty two pans. She placed chunks of potato, sprinkled with dried oregano, into the same pan as the roast. Due to the longer cooking time of the roast, the potatoes were crisp and overcooked by her standards, but I thought they were terrific. Had she been anyone else, she might have surmised that I was making fun of her. I was not. These potatoes became a family favorite, much to her bewilderment. Yet, while I did not know it then, the potatoes could have been improved with rosemary. The only rosemary we may have had at home was probably in one of those gift spice racks somebody inevitably gave you back then. Like the dried marjoram, parsley, and fennel seeds, it basked in the open light of the kitchen until its dubious flavor was indistinguishable from any of the others. And so it was many years before I discovered that fresh rosemary is one of those gifts of Nature that can set the world right when it has gone out of kilter.

Next to fresh basil, fresh rosemary is my favorite herb. In Jim Jarmusch's *Down by Law*, three convicts escape from a southern prison. Famished and on the run in the backwoods and bayous of Louisiana, Bob, played by Roberto Benigni, snares and roasts a rabbit. Hungry as they are, Tom Waits and John Lurie gaze in great distaste at the charred rabbit. Benigni, not realizing that the men are actually repelled by the prospect of eating a rabbit, apologizes and says that it needs some *rosmarino*—rosemary. If there is a part of Italy that does not relish the pungent green leaves of the rosemary plant, I do not know it. From the top of "the boot" to the toe, the uses of rosemary are as diversified as the regions that use it to enhance their cooking. But back to the potatoes. Here are two versions. The first is inspired by the white wines of Tuscany, and the second is definitely the progeny of rustic Sicily.

Tipsy Tuscan Roasted Potatoes

SERVES 4

1½ pounds Yukon gold potatoes, scrubbed, or peeled if you
   prefer
2 tablespoons full-bodied extra-virgin olive oil
Coarse or kosher salt and freshly ground pepper to taste
1 cup dry white wine
2 tablespoons coarsely chopped fresh rosemary

1. Preheat the oven to 375 degrees. Cut the potatoes into ⅛-inch slices and soak in cold water for about 10 minutes. Drain and dry.

2. In a large bowl, toss the potatoes with the olive oil and salt and pepper. Spread the potatoes out on a large, wide, shallow roasting pan, making sure that the oil has coated the bottom of the pan. Pour the wine around the potatoes and sprinkle on the rosemary.

3. Bake, loosely covered with foil, for about 15 minutes. Raise the heat to 400 degrees. Remove the foil and continue baking until the potatoes are just crisp around the edges and the wine has evaporated, another 15 to 20 minutes.

Sicilian-Style Rosemary Potatoes with Black Olives and Cherry Tomatoes

SERVES 4

1½ pounds tiny new red potatoes or larger ones cut in half
1 tablespoon extra-virgin olive oil (preferably Sicilian)
2 tablespoons coarsely chopped fresh rosemary
1 tablespoon chopped garlic
Coarse or kosher salt and freshly ground pepper to taste
16 small cherry or grape tomatoes
16 Sicilian oil-cured black olives (or other oil-cured black olives such as Gaeta or niçoise olives), pitted or whole
2 tablespoons coarsely chopped fresh flat-leaf parsley

1. Parboil the potatoes for about 5 minutes. When cool enough to handle, gently smack them with the back of a large knife or a frying pan until they just slightly crack.

2. Heat the olive oil in a large skillet over medium-high heat and add the potatoes, stirring to coat them. Add the rosemary, garlic, and salt and pepper and cook, continuing to stir the potatoes, until they begin to crisp, 10 to 15 minutes.

3. Stir in the tomatoes and the olives and cook for another 2 minutes, or until the tomato skins begin to wrinkle. Sprinkle with chopped parsley and serve immediately.

Twice-Cooked Green Beans and Potatoes with Tomato Sauce

SERVES 4 AS A SIDE DISH

This was a dish that Nanny never made when her husband was alive. I suspect that she was longing for the foods that he was not so crazy about. I don't know if this was one of her favorite dishes, but after I sampled it, it became one of mine. It is so outrageously easy that I would have bet that even my mother could have made it if she tried—except it is made with something that was a novelty in our home: fresh green beans. If you can find the thinner *haricots verts* (French-style green beans) they are even better in this dish.

> 1 large russet potato, scrubbed (peeled if desired) and cut into
>   1-inch cubes
> Salt for the water, plus coarse or kosher salt to taste
> 1 pound green beans
> ¼ cup extra-virgin olive oil
> 1½ teaspoons chopped garlic
> ¾ pound of ripe tomatoes, seeded and diced, or grape or
>   cherry tomatoes, halved
> Freshly ground pepper to taste
> ½ cup freshly torn basil leaves

1. Place the potato in a 2- to 3-quart pot, and just cover with cold water. Salt the water and bring it to a boil. Reduce the heat to medium-low and simmer the potato until you can just pierce the cubes with a fork, 15 to 20 minutes. Drain from the pot with a slotted spoon, rinse, and set them aside. Keep the water for the beans.

2. Remove the stem ends from the beans and cook in the same salted boiling water until barely tender. Drain and place in a cold-water bath until needed. Cut the beans in half.

3. Heat the oil over medium heat in a large pan. Add garlic and sauté until it becomes golden, but not brown. Add the tomatoes and salt and pepper and raise heat to medium-high until the tomatoes' liquid begins to evaporate, about 10 minutes. Gently break up the tomatoes with the back of a wooden spoon while cooking. Lastly, add the beans and potatoes to the sauce and stir. Heat until the beans are just cooked through, about 2 minutes. Transfer to a wide bowl and stir in the basil. This dish may be served warm or at room temperature as a salad.

Pears Stuffed with Gorgonzola

SERVES 4

My father was a fiend for fresh fruit. Perhaps he knew that nobody could ruin it for him. After a partially eaten meal, he would relax a bit, and then eventually raid the fruit bowl. This love of fruit, of course, is universal in Italy, and the country's more than 25 million acres of farmland yield a vast amount and wide variety of fruits. The people of Lombardy are no exception; they try to have fruit at least once a day. Cosmopolitan Milan is on par with the fastest paced cities in the world, but there is always time for fruit. And there is always time for leisurely cooking. The Milanese like to point out that to mollify the hustle and bustle of their daily urban affairs, they take time out for relaxing by cooking and dining. Milan in particular is rightly known for its savory, slow-cooked soups, braises, and, in particular, its *ossobuco*.

To complement their hearty dishes, the Milanese like to balance their meals with fresh fruit. Unlike my father's love for unadorned fresh fruit, the Milanese often embellish their fruit with other staples, including cheese and even butter. The latter may come as a surprise, but the people of Milan maintain that butter was first created outside their city and was enjoyed by no lesser personage than Julius Caesar. The following pear dish is a perfect pairing of tastes and textures. I would recommend Champagne with this dish, but an Aperol on the rocks with a dash of Prosecco is also a fitting choice.

    4 small, firm, ripe pears, preferably Bosc
    2 tablespoons freshly squeezed lemon juice
    2 ounces Gorgonzola *dolce* at room temperature
    2 tablespoons unsalted butter at room temperature
    2 tablespoons crushed pistachio nuts

1. Carefully peel the pears, leaving the stems attached. Cut them in half lengthwise and scoop out the seeds and just enough pulp to allow for a small hollow for the cheese and butter mixture. Rub the pears with the lemon juice to prevent discoloration.

2. In a small bowl, cream the Gorgonzola and the butter together with a fork. Scrape the side of the bowl to incorporate the cheese and butter well until the mixture is soft and fluffy. Fill the hollows of the pear halves with the cheese mixture and carefully press the two halves of the pears back together again. Roll the pears in the crushed pistachio nuts and set them on a serving dish. Cover with plastic wrap and refrigerate until the cheese mixture is firm, at least 2 hours.

Pasta

Life is a combination of magic and pasta.
—FEDERICO FELLINI

The only time I heard the word "pasta" as a boy was in reference to *"pasta fazool."* Then there is the old joke: Q. What is the fastest car in Italy? A. The Fazool. No one can go pasta Fazool. The pastas almost exclusively boiled and sauced were spaghetti and ravioli. In rare instances there were wagon wheels—*ruote di carro.* Shells, *ziti,* and *rigatoni* were always baked, but usually by someone else's family. I certainly had heard of linguine, seeing it on menus served with clam sauce, but my mother was faithful to her beloved Ronzoni "Italian Style" spaghetti. Shapes such as *penne, orecchiette,* and *farfalle,* which are quite common today, were absent from our home. During the 1950s, Ronzoni did have more than fifty varieties of macaroni, but few found their way to the shelves of our local King Kullen supermarket. Until fairly recently, true Italian pasta could be tracked down only in Italian markets or specialty shops. I was thrilled about a dozen years ago when our Stop & Shop began to carry De Cecco pasta. I was subsequently crestfallen when they soon ceased. I asked the store manager why, and he told me that I was probably the only one who bought it. Happily that has all changed, and numerous Italian brands are now close at hand.

The extraordinary range of names, shapes, and sizes can approach the whimsical. *Strozzapreti* are so-named "priest stranglers" after an incident involving a gluttonous cleric and this pasta. *Farfalle* are so named because they resemble butterflies. *Eliche* are "screws," *fusilli* are "spindles," *radiatori* are "radiators," *lancette* are "clock hands," and *gomiti* are "crankshafts," just to name a few other colorful translations. If you cannot find more obscure varieties like *paccheri* or *fusilli con buco*, there is always the Internet. Eataly. com alone offers a selection of about a hundred dried pastas. (This is practically nothing compared to the latest "pasta counter's" counts, which estimate as many as thirteen hundred individual shapes.) But once again, read the fine print on the package. Barilla touts itself as "Italy's #1 brand of pasta." As for Italy's #1 Barilla pasta sold in the States, if you look at the side of the box in your supermarket, you will see that the pasta you are buying in America hails from towns like Ames, Iowa, or Avon, New York. For a fun and informative tour through the gamut of hundreds of tubes, twists, and folds, I would recommend Caz Hildebrand and Jacob Kennedy's *The Geometry of Pasta*.

Despite its popularity throughout history, pasta was also often as reviled as it was praised. The zealous fifteenth-century monk Girolomo Savonarola—famed for bringing on the "bonfire of the vanities"—railed against it. Julia della Croce cites one fiery sermon: "It's not enough for you to eat your pasta fried. No! You think you have to add garlic to it, and when you eat ravioli, it's not enough to boil it in a pot and eat it in its juice, you have to fry it in another pan and cover it with cheese!" He was fittingly fried himself, as he was burned at the stake in 1498. Italians will go only so far in sanctioning self-denial of pasta. Fast-forward to the early twentieth century when the futurist poet Filippo Marinetti put in his two lire. Pasta, he asserted, made people heavy in both body and spirit, turned them sour and pessimistic, and robbed them of their creative impulse. The relinquishment of pasta wasn't merely a matter of individual salvation. He even made it a matter of patriotism, arguing that the abolition of pasta would liberate Italy from the despotism of expensive foreign grain. He is quoted as saying, "Spaghetti is no food for fighters." Mussolini agreed, and the fascist dictator considered banning pasta consumption entirely. This was reason enough for him to be shot, kicked, and spat upon, and his body hung upside down on meat hooks from the roof of an Esso gas station.

In Italy today, pasta is like a near-sacred object for most people. It is fed to babies as soon as they can take in solids. In Italian households, its place as a first dish at lunch or dinner is practically set in stone, and the most traditional pasta makers want to retain the integrity of their products. And so there is pasta; there is Italian pasta; and then there is Italian pasta from Gragnano. In Gragnano, a small town near the Amalfi Coast, this famous pasta capital boasted almost two hundred pasta factories during the town's manufacturing heyday a century ago. Gragnanesi assert that the spring water, mountain air, and sunshine of their area combine to make their local pastas deservedly famous throughout Italy. The Cooperativa di Pasta Gragnano, representing small producers in the area, declares that the dough should be made solely from Italian wheat and be pushed through perforated bronze plates to mold it. The resulting strands, sheets, and elegant shapes must be dried at temperatures no higher than 122 degrees because, in their view, higher temperatures "burn" the dough. Daniel Williams wrote a piece for the *Washington Post*, entitled "Gragnano's Crisis in a Pasta Pot" (January 19, 2005). In it he pointed out that the Gragnano Pasta City Consortium of ten large manufacturers has argued for somewhat looser manufacturing rules, but Antonio Marchetti, the cooperative's president, argues that "Gragnano pasta must be different from all other pasta to preserve the prestige of the name. Dilute the quality means to dilute the value."

Purists maintain that the best Italian dried pasta is extruded through bronze dies to create a rough, porous surface. When cooked, the rough surface of the pasta allows full absorption of added sauces. Long, dried pasta wants a great deal of boiling water—about a gallon per pound (with about 2 tablespoons of salt added only after the water comes to a full boil)—but shorter shapes like *farfalle* can cook in slightly less water. And always save some of the pasta water in case your sauce needs thinning out. As to which Italian pasta is best, my only advice here is that you try different brands to see which one suits your taste and budget. Also be wary of the cooking time on the package since the pasta makers do not know what kind of a range, pot, water, and so on, you are using. At up to $5 a pound, and sometimes more, artisanal pasta is an investment.

Moreover, it is not out of ignorance that Afeltra Pasta group of Naples suggests a cooking time of between 13 and 16 minutes for their *fusilli con buco* (long *fusilli* with a "mouth," or hole down the center), but the package also advises testing for doneness. In fact, my *fusilli* was done in 9 minutes. All ranges and stovetops have different BTUs, and a Viking range will heat the water faster and maintain a steady, rapid boil compared to, say, a camp two-burner. Start tasting the pasta before the recommended time. Eventually you will also get a sense of near-doneness by watching the change in color. Should you add oil to the water? Don't even dare ask! Stirring immediately and then occasionally will prevent the pasta from sticking. Finally, by no means rinse the pasta after you drain it. This will wash out the starch and much of the flavor.

As for fresh pasta, there are two types of fresh pasta: *pasta liscia* (smooth pasta) and *pasta ripiena* (stuffed pasta), the latter made by shaping the dough into pockets of various shapes and filling them with a variety of ingredients. Typical types of *pasta liscia* include *pappardelle, fettuccine, orecchiette, trenette, tagliatelle,* and *taglierini,* the latter two types are derivatives of the Italian verb *tagliare* (from "to cut"). Pasta is also cut into square shapes, like Liguria's *lasagne.* *Pasta ripiena* is far more diverse in that not only are there myriad shapes, but also the pasta is stuffed with any number of different fillings. Initially, stuffed pasta was found predominantly throughout northern and central Italy. This is because pasta needs eggs to strengthen the dough, allow it to be pliable, and create elasticity. Prior to the unification of Italy, eggs were a precious commodity in

the comparatively poor south. Therefore, *pasta ripiena* was not often found in the more humble kitchens until later. Some well-known *paste ripiene* include square and ruffled edge *agnolotti* from Piedmont; *agnolini*, half-moons from Emilia-Romagna; *tortelli*, large squares found in central Italy; and *cappelletti*, small rings of pasta from Modena.

Homemade pasta is not as difficult to make as most people think. Unless you go to a specialty shop, where you will pay top dollar for freshly made pasta, no store-bought, packaged "fresh" pasta can compare to the silken texture of freshly made pasta. The drawback is that you need time and a pasta machine. A sturdy manual machine will only set you back about $40.

We may then ask, what wine should one drink with pasta? Since even the old rule of red wine with meat and white wine with fish has been challenged, so, too, should you consider which wine will be in harmony with your dish. As a loose rule of thumb for tomato-based pasta, since tomatoes are acidic, you want to avoid anything too tannic. Reds such as Montepulciano, Barbera, Chianti, or even an old-vine Zinfandel pair nicely. Lighter sauces would call for a buttery Chardonnay or a soft Pinot Grigio.

A Word About Eating Pasta

As I mentioned earlier, it is pure hearsay that Marco Polo brought the concept of the pasta noodle back with him from his travels in China. According to Silvano Serventi and Françoise Sabban, in their *Pasta: The Story of a Universal Food*, the legend originated with the *Macaroni Journal*, published by an association of food industries with the goal of promoting the use of pasta in the United States. John Thorne in *Outlaw Cook* wryly pondered that "[Marco Polo] might have done his fellow Italians a good turn instead and brought them chopsticks—those simple, useful, egalitarian eating tools, so perfect for catching up and conveying noodles to the mouth." Indeed, the earliest images of Italians eating spaghetti show them eschewing forks as well, as the food is eaten with the hands alone. The hungry pasta maven is generally shown hoisting a fistful of gnarly noodles high above his head and draping it down into his mouth. These images persist right into the nineteenth century. Julia della Croce's *Pasta Classica* is filled with some illustrations that border on the hilarious.

As for the fork, another invention whose history is as open to speculation as pasta's, it did not begin to gain wide acceptance in Italy until well into the fourteenth century. And even then the eating of pasta by the well-to-do was still a hand-to-mouth operation. Initially flour was very expensive. As pasta became more affordable and the lower classes took to gorging on it, the upper classes set to distinguish themselves from the masses by preferring utensils for eating their noodles. Whether or not to use a spoon to twirl your spaghetti, that is another bone of contention entirely. For most educated Italians, though, using a spoon is not a far step from the crassness of using your hands. Whatever your choice, Sydney Clark in *All the Best in Italy* has perhaps the final word on the matter: "It is impossible to be dainty eating spaghetti." I wonder what Sophia Loren, who said, "Everything you see I owe to spaghetti," would say to that.

Then there is the question: How much pasta should be allotted per person? A common saying in Italian households is "A fistful for everyone, and one for the pot." Clearly there is no consensus on amounts, nor should there be. It really comes down to how much you want to eat. For my wife and me, I simply divide the package in half, cooking half and saving the other for another meal. Depending on the thickness of the pasta, there is almost always some left over. This would mean that we consume between 3 and 4 ounces for our meal. Americans tend not to eat pasta as a first course, but since many Italians do, in the recipes that follow I have given proportions for both according to my present taste. Rather than be pedantic about it, I have therefore listed the amount for each recipe as "serves roughly."

Cacio e Pepe

SERVES ROUGHLY 6 AS A FIRST COURSE

AND 4 AS A MAIN COURSE

This is yet another dish that I conceivably cannot live without. Naturally, this pasta would be impossible to make properly with the aforementioned worthless powder we called pepper in my parents' house. Moreover, as simple as this dish is to make, for some reason in our house, pasta sauces needed to take hours. The notion of a quick pasta was as remote as the Hebrides.

Cacio e Pepe, or very pure and simply "cheese and pepper," is exactly that: pure and simple at its best. In fact, this classic Roman dish is so simple that almost anyone who makes it these days wants to add something else to it. You may too, but try it in its basic, unadorned form first. For this dish, all you need is spaghetti, water, pepper, and cheese (salt for the boiling water does not count!). The majority of recipes will add olive oil or butter as well as Parmigiano. Romans would consider this an abomination. Initially the pasta was not completely drained of the cooking water. This accounted for its slight creaminess. Other cooks will drain it dry and bathe it with the fat rendered from *guanciale* or pancetta before tossing it with the pepper and cheese. John Thorne in his *Outlaw Cook* recalls the Roman-born Los Angeles restaurateur Mauro Vincenti, who does exactly that; but in addition, he maintains that the spaghetti should be cooked filo de fero (iron string), which is firmer than al dente. Typically, the pepper was pounded out in a mortar, but some of today's pepper grinders, such as the Unicorn Magnum Plus, made in Nantucket, are excellent for a superbly coarse-ground pepper. Here is the recipe in its unvarnished original form. As they used to say in that old television commercial, "Try it. You'll like it!"

1 pound spaghetti

1 cup grated Pecorino Romano (at least!), with more for serving

1 tablespoon very coarsely ground, or crushed, black pepper,
or more to taste
Nothing else

Bring 4 quarts of water to a boil. Salt the water, add the spaghetti, and cook until al dente. Reserve some of the cooking water. Drain the pasta to a serving dish, leaving some of the cooking water clinging to it. Add the cheese and black pepper. Blend slowly so that the cheese does not congeal. Stir in just enough of the cooking liquid to give the pasta a creamy texture. Serve at once with extra cheese and pepper.

Spaghetti con Aglio, Olio, e Peperoncino

By the late 1980s I had sampled much of what would be called Italian home cooking in Italy. Until then, though, I had not had the opportunity to actually have an Italian meal cooked in an Italian home. My first experience was at the home of Alessandra Baldini's parents in Bologna. Ali is married to a dear friend of many years, Joe Alchermes. Joe and I went to graduate school together, and we still share a liking for martinis, the Marx Brothers, and those "damned" Yankees. Unlike my home of ersatz Italian food, however, his family in Brooklyn maintained tradition—a tradition that was equally evident and going strong at its source in Italy.

Our first course in Bologna was a truly amazing dish: spaghetti with garlic, olive oil, lemon zest, and breadcrumbs. Since the dish more probably originates from the more southerly regions of Italy, the abundance of garlic in this recipe should not be a complete surprise. Skip the lemon zest and breadcrumbs and you have just garlic and oil, which may be one of the first pasta sauces ever conceived. Giuliano

Bugialli in *Bugialli on Pasta* asserted that this almost primitive fare is still found throughout Italy, and it is reasonable "to regard it as possibly the oldest of all dressings." That alone necessitates its inclusion here. Personally, I like to add a healthy dash of crushed red pepper. As for grated cheese, Bugialli commands that grated cheese is never added to any aglio-olio presentation.

1 pound spaghetti

¼ cup fruity extra-virgin olive oil, plus more for serving

6 fresh, plump cloves of garlic, thinly sliced with stinger removed

Dash of crushed red pepper (optional)

Chopped fresh parsley (optional)

Freshly ground pepper to taste

1. Bring 4 quarts of water to a boil. Salt the water, add the spaghetti, and cook until barely al dente. While the pasta is cooking, heat the oil over medium-low in a pan large enough to contain the pasta, and add the garlic and (if using it) the crushed red pepper. Stir the garlic until it begins to color, but not brown. Drain pasta and reserve 1 cup of the cooking liquid.

2. Add ½ cup of the pasta cooking water to the garlic mixture in the pan and reduce it over high heat by about half. Add the pasta and stir vigorously. Slowly add the reserved pasta water as needed to finish cooking the pasta and create a creamy sauce. Serve with the parsley and the freshly ground pepper and more olive oil to taste.

Tagliatelle with Lamb Ragù

SERVES ROUGHLY 6 AS A FIRST COURSE
AND 4 AS A MAIN COURSE

According to Lynne Rossetto Kasper in the public radio show *The Splendid Table*, the earliest documented recipe for a meat-based sauce (*ragù*) served with pasta comes from late-eighteenth-century Imola, near Bologna. My "Bolognese" calls for ground lamb instead of the traditional quartet of beef, veal, pork, and chicken livers. This single alteration adds a rich, slightly gamey flavor that would be impossible to achieve using any other single meat—for me, that is. Add the fresh rosemary to this and you will have such a rich *ragù* that you may want to eat it by itself. Apart from the lamb and rosemary—which I admit is a lot—this recipe and its method are much closer to what you will find in Bologna than what you'll find in cookbooks and food magazines here. My first taste of a true *ragù* was in Bologna, and it was a revelation. To start, there is only a hint of tomato in the form of tomato paste in this dish. I suspect that adding up to an entire can of tomatoes in Americanized versions may have been an attempt to adapt this time-honored classic to the American palate.

Nevertheless, Bolognese is a meat sauce, not a tomato sauce. The whole point of a meat sauce is to taste the meat and the flavor it develops over its long cooking time. Secondly, the wine used for this sauce in Italy is white, not red. Some may disagree with me, but I think that the white gives a subtlety to the sauce, whereas red overwhelms it. Save the red to drink with the finished pasta. The white wine they use in the dish in Emilia-Romagna is the local Trebbiano. This should come as no surprise since that is the grape whose must is used for the local balsamic vinegar. Even if you decide to use beef and pork instead of lamb (or even goat meat, as I have done with success), the recipe that follows will serve as a model for a fairly authentic

Bolognese. I say "fairly" because the dish's regional variations may include lemon zest and mushrooms.

Being a meaty dish, Bolognese calls for a "meaty" red wine. You can run the gamut from Montepulciano d'Abruzzo and Chianti Classico to Valpolicella or a reserve Malbec.

Note: *This sauce may also be served with any baked pasta, and it is ideal for cannelloni or lasagne. It is also works well in a risotto.*

½ pound *pancetta*, diced

3 tablespoons extra-virgin olive oil

½ cup diced onion

½ cup diced carrot

½ cup diced celery

1 pound ground or minced lamb

½ teaspoon crushed red pepper

½ cup dry white wine

2 tablespoons double-concentrated Italian (or Muir Glen)
   tomato paste, diluted in 1 cup beef stock

Several fresh branches of rosemary

1 cup whole milk

Coarse or kosher salt and freshly ground black pepper, to taste

½ cup heavy cream

1 pound *tagliatelle*, preferably fresh, but dried will suffice

½ cup grated Parmigiano for serving

1. In a 3-quart saucier or heavy saucepan, sauté the *pancetta* in olive oil over medium heat until the *pancetta* begins to render its fat, about 5 minutes. Stir in the onion, carrot, and celery and continue sautéing until the vegetables have softened, about another 4 minutes. Blend in the lamb and the crushed red pepper and brown the meat, breaking it up with a wooden spoon, until it has uniformly lost its rawness, 7 to 10 minutes.

2. Stir in the wine into the lamb and reduce the liquid by half. Add the diluted tomato paste, toss in the rosemary, and reduce the heat to the barest simmer (a flame tamer may help if your stove is too hot). Partially cover the pan and cook slowly for 2 hours, stirring occasionally and adding the milk a little at a time. After about 1½ hours add the salt and pepper to taste.

3. Meanwhile in a small pot simmer the cream until it has reduced slightly, about 3 minutes. Cover and set aside.

4. When the sauce is nearly done, bring 4 quarts of water to a boil. Salt the water, add the *tagliatelle*, and cook until al dente. While the pasta is cooking, remove the remains of the rosemary branches (the leaves will have blended into the sauce), and stir the cream into the *ragù*. Drain the pasta thoroughly. Toss the pasta with the hot *ragù* and serve with the grated Parmigiano.

Bucatini all'Amatriciana

SERVES ROUGHLY 6 AS A FIRST COURSE
AND 4 AS A MAIN COURSE

I have already mentioned early on that when Ada Boni's groundbreaking *Italian Regional Cooking* was published here in 1969, it was a turning point for Italian cookbooks. For a nation of individuals who were only accustomed to red sauce, *Arancini di Riso, Gnocchi di Polenta, Scacciata con Caciocavallo* cheese (a Sicilian bread pie) were newcomers to our shore. Far surpassing her revered *The Talisman Italian Cook Book* of 1950, it was a virtual tour through all of the Italian culinary landscape from the countryside to the seacoasts—in full color. Still, she did have to account for some ingredients that were not to be seen except perhaps in a very special Italian market. And even then, due to FDA regulations, the products would have been made here. One such ingredient is *guanciale*, the jowl of Cinta Senese pigs. Thus her *Spaghetti al Guanciale* was translated as Spaghetti with Bacon. Updated recipes have substituted *pancetta*, but in the late '60s, even that now-common meat was rarely seen. She also replaced the unfamiliar *bucatini* with the ubiquitous spaghetti.

Spaghetti noodles, however, are no substitute for *bucatini*. The latter are a thicker noodle with a hole down the center. The name itself comes from *buco* (hole), and that hole down the center allows the pasta to cook rather quickly from the inside out. What I do find odd about Boni's use of bacon in lieu of *guanciale*, though, is that she does have recipes that include pig ears and pig trotters. Perhaps the editor simply thought that no one would ever make those, so why bother substituting ingredients (and what would you substitute for a pig ear anyway?).

Although one may find this dish in Umbria and the Marches, like *Cacio e Pepe* and *Spaghetti alla Carbonara*, *Bucatini all'Amatriciana* is distinctly Roman. Once *cucina povera*, peasant food, these dishes have been gentrified to include the finest tomatoes and the best cheeses. But gentrification comes with a price, as your bill at any upscale Roman menu will bear out. To make this dish the authentic Roman way, you will need *guanciale*, as even pancetta does not have its buttery quality. Unless you live in New York or another major city, guanciale is still difficult to find. Your best bet is an online purveyor (see Mail-Order Sources). Note that garlic was a later addition, and I have therefore listed it as an optional ingredient. In summer you may also substitute fresh tomatoes for the canned variety.

1 tablespoon extra-virgin olive oil
¼ pound *guanciale*, thinly sliced and cut into ½-inch pieces
1 medium onion cut lengthwise in half and then sliced into thin half-moons
1½ teaspoons minced garlic (optional)
½ teaspoon crushed red pepper, or to taste
1 28-ounce can whole peeled tomatoes
Coarse or kosher salt and plenty of freshly ground pepper to taste
1 pound *bucatini*
½ cup grated Pecorino Romano, with more for serving

1. Heat the oil over medium heat in a large skillet that will hold all the pasta. Add the *guanciale* and sauté until it is beginning to brown, 5 to 6 minutes. Be careful, *guanciale* is very delicate and can burn easily. Remove the *guanciale* to a paper towel. Add the onion and garlic to the fat and sauté over medium heat until transparent. Sprinkle in hot pepper and stir in the *guanciale*.

2. Pour the tomato liquid from the can into your pot, and then gradually crush the tomatoes, pouring more liquid into the pot as you go. Bring to a boil, immediately turn the heat to low, and simmer until the sauce has become somewhat concentrated, about 20 minutes. Add the salt and pepper about halfway through.

3. When the sauce is nearly done, bring 4 quarts of water to a boil. Salt the water, add the pasta, and cook for about a minute short of the recommended time. Drain the pasta and add it to the skillet. Continue heating for another minute until the pasta is well-coated, about 5 minutes. Fold in the ¼ cup of cheese. Serve immediately with more cheese on the side.

Spaghetti alla Carbonara

SERVES ROUGHLY 6 AS A FIRST COURSE
AND 4 AS A MAIN COURSE

I have included *Spaghetti alla Carbonara* if only to return it to its legitimate Roman heritage. I know I'm not one to talk, but as delicious as the variations may be, sometimes we can lose sight of the original, and we should revisit it. I'm guessing, but I don't think it was Ada Boni, Marcella Hazan, or, for that matter, any great Italian chef who popularized *Spaghetti alla Carbonara* in the New World. The humorist Calvin Trillin may have introduced it as a joke. In 1983 he initiated a campaign to have Thanksgiving changed to "*Spaghetti*

alla Carbonara Day." The holiday did not catch on—or at least I don't think it did—but due to his writing and his appearance on television and radio shows, the dish did.

From its humble origins of meat, cheese, and eggs in oil, carbonara recipes have deviated to include butter, wine onions, garlic, peas, broccoli, mushrooms, cream, rosemary, and even jalapeño peppers. In the case of *Spaghetti alla Carbonara*, purportedly created as a quick, hearty meal for Italian charcoal workers, simplicity carries the day. There have been many warnings about contamination from the *Salmonella Enteritidis* bacteria from fresh raw eggs, but you cannot make this dish without them. Just as with *Caesar Salad*, organic free-range eggs are the way to go.

Some say that the dish was named for the *carbonari* of Rome—the charcoal burners who produced charcoal from wood for everything from medicinal cures to fuel for the blacksmith's forge (and, of course, the barbecue). Others say that it was created as a tribute to the *Carbonari*, a secret society prominent in the early, repressed stages of Italian unification. Others yet claim it was named for coal miners, while another source maintains that the name actually refers to the black pasta made from squid ink by the ancient Romans. According to Alan Davidson, in his prodigious *Oxford Companion to Food*, *Spaghetti alla Carbonara* was invented in 1944 when many Italians were eating eggs and bacon supplied by American occupation troops. In other words, nobody really knows.

Carbonara lends itself to a variety of wines, white and red. You could go with an Amarone or Chianti, but an Orvieto or a light-bodied Chardonnay would go well if you prefer whites. For something completely different, the slight sweetness and fizz of a Lambrusco will help cut through the fat of the *Carbonara* sauce.

2 tablespoons extra-virgin olive oil

¼ pound *guanciale*, thinly sliced and cut into ¼-inch pieces

2 teaspoons coarsely cracked fresh pepper

1 pound spaghetti

½ cup freshly grated Parmigiano, plus more for serving

4 egg yolks, lightly beaten

Coarse or kosher salt to taste

1. Heat a small skillet over medium-low heat and add the olive oil. Add the *guanciale* and sauté until it is barely beginning to brown, 5 to 6 minutes. Stir in the pepper and cook for another minute. Transfer to a large bowl or serving dish and let cool slightly.

2. Bring 4 quarts of water to a boil. Salt the water, add the pasta and cook until al dente. While the pasta is cooking, add the Parmigiano, eggs, and salt to the *guanciale*. Drain pasta, reserving ¼ cup pasta water. Toss the pasta with the sauce, and slowly add the reserved water until the mixture is creamy (you may not need all of the water). Serve, allowing your guests to sprinkle on more cheese and black pepper to taste.

Rotini with 'Nduja and Cherry Tomatoes

SERVES ROUGHLY 6 AS A FIRST COURSE
AND 4 AS A MAIN COURSE

Once again, it is odd that some of the foods that graced the southern Italian table not only were unknown to my family, but were never even mentioned. Calabrian hot pepper in oil is one, and another is *'nduja*. Pronounced *en-DOO-ya*, *nduja* of Spilinga is a spreadable cured meat or salami made with pork, salt, herbs, sometimes wine, and the famous Calabrian chilies, making it quite a spicy, if not fiery cured meat. It was born as a humble ingredient prepared by farmers in order to use the remaining parts of the pig. The name *'nduja* comes from the French word *andouille*, which means "sausage." The original provenance of this humble ingredient is the Calabrian town of Vibo Valentia, but nowadays *'nduja* is produced throughout the region. Although it is still somewhat foreign to the American table, it has caught on in

Britain as the latest Italian food trend. It is a versatile foodstuff that can be enjoyed simply spread on crusty bread, but because of its ability to melt when heated, it is ideal for paring with pasta. You probably will not find it locally, but you can order it online from Boccalone or the Underground Food Collective of Wisconsin (see Mail-Order Sources). What I also like about this recipe is that it is startlingly simple to prepare. I use the term *rotini* here because that is its most popular name in America, but the pasta also goes by the names *ruote*, *rotine*, and *rotelle*, all of which basically translate as "wheels."

> 2 tablespoons extra-virgin olive oil
> 1½ teaspoons minced garlic
> ¼ cup finely chopped shallots
> 3 ounces *'nduja* (removed from casing, if any)
> ¼ pound cherry tomatoes, halved
> Coarse or kosher salt to taste
> 1 pound *rotini* or other pasta of choice
> Chopped parsley for serving

1. In a large skillet, heat oil over medium heat until shimmering. Add garlic and shallots and cook until golden, but not brown, about 5 minutes. Add the *'nduja* to mixture, breaking it up with a wooden spoon, and stir until melted. Stir in the tomatoes and salt and continue cooking until the tomatoes begin to break down, about another 5 minutes. Turn the heat to low, just to keep the sauce heated while the pasta cooks.

2. While the sauce is cooking, bring 4 quarts of water to a boil. Salt the water, add the pasta, and cook until al dente. Drain the pasta and reserve about ¼ cup pasta water. Add the pasta to the sauce and stir, adding some reserved pasta water if the mixture is too dry. Top with chopped parsley and serve.

Pappardelle with Spicy Sausage Sauce

SERVES ROUGHLY 6 AS A FIRST COURSE
AND 4 AS A MAIN COURSE

I do not know why, but my mother rarely served sausage. When she did it was usually pan-fried and tossed whole or in halves into a red sauce. Otherwise it was Jones breakfast sausage. I have no way of knowing, short of a Ouija board, but I do think that Nanny may have put some finely crumbled hot sausage into her sauce to give it a kick. Italian butcher shops throughout Italy boast of their sausage making. Every province in Emilia-Romagna has its own special salumi. From the sweet (never hot) cotechino of Emilia-Romagna to the *salsiccia Napoletana piccante*, a spicy dry sausage from Naples, the variety of sausages seems endless. Yet one rarely finds them incorporated in traditional pasta sauces.

Loving hot sausage as I do, I have no problem making a sauce with plenty of sausages. One snowy evening some years back, a friend of mine was very lucky to get a seat at the bar of New York's Rao's. I stress lucky because the co-owner, Frank Pellegrino, has received the nickname "Frankie No" for the number of people he turns away every day. My friend described the dish that he had that night. It was an incredible spicy sausage over pappardelle. It may have been only the day after he told me about it that I began experimenting to duplicate it. This is certainly not Rao's, but it is my version. I like it spicy, so I add extra hot pepper as well. The name for the pasta is derived from the Italian pappare—"to scarf down"—something that will be in order after tasting these luscious ribbons.

¼ cup extra-virgin olive oil
¾ cup chopped onion

4 hot Italian sausages, casing removed

Crushed red pepper (optional)

½ cups dry white wine

1 28-ounce can of whole peeled tomatoes

½ teaspoon dried oregano

Coarse or kosher salt and freshly ground black pepper to taste

1 pound dried *pappardelle*

Freshly grated Pecorino Romano to taste for finishing and
serving

A handful of fresh basil leaves, torn into ½-inch pieces

1. Heat the oil in a large skillet over medium-high heat. Add the onions and sauté until soft, about 4 minutes.

2. While the onions are cooking, add the sausage and crushed red pepper, if using, to the onion, breaking up the sausage with a wooden spoon as you go. Sauté until the sausage begins to brown, about 7 minutes.

3. Turn the heat to high and stir in the wine and stir to combine. Boil until the wine has reduced by a third. Pour the tomato liquid from the can into your pot, and then gradually crush the tomatoes, pouring more liquid into the pot as you go. Bring to a boil, immediately turn the heat to low, and simmer until the sauce has become somewhat concentrated, about 20 minutes.

4. While the sauce is cooking, bring 4 quarts of water to a boil. Salt the water, add the pasta, and cook for about a minute short of the recommended time.

5. Drain the *pappardelle* and return it to its cooking pot. Quickly stir in about ½ cup sauce and turn the heat to medium-high. Toss the pasta with a wooden spoon until it is well coated, about 1 minute. Remove the pasta from the heat and pour it into a large bowl, spooning the rest of the sauce over the top. Stir in about 1 tablespoon of the Pecorino Romano and sprinkle the pasta with the torn basil leaves. Serve immediately, passing the grated cheese.

Pasta with Mortadella Sauce

SERVES ROUGHLY 6 AS A FIRST COURSE
AND 4 AS A MAIN COURSE

John Willoughby and Chris Schlesinger have included several recipes for grilled or fried bologna in their inventive cookbooks. The first time I saw this I thought that it must be some kind of inside joke on their part—until I tried one of the recipes. I later learned that Italians are no strangers when it comes to cooking true bologna, mortadella. Made from finely ground pork laced with spices, and then larded, mortadella sausages can weigh up to 180 pounds. The name most likely is rooted in the word *mortaio*, since the ingredients were mashed together in a large mortar to make the sausage.

Although most of the Italian cookbooks I own use mortadella in cooking, not one offered a recipe for a mortadella sauce. Therefore the following recipe is the result of much trial and error. Should I just use the mortadella and no pork? Do I skip the canned tomatoes and add milk, as in a Bolognese? One can now purchase real Italian mortadella in specialty shops or online. The major exporter is the company Parmacotto, and it is definitely worth seeking out to make this unusual pasta dish. Otherwise, the American-made mortadella from Fratelli Beretta is available from many online sources. I especially like the 1-pound mini mortadella because it is just enough of the delectable pork product to keep one from pigging out.

2 tablespoons extra-virgin olive oil

½ pound piece of mortadella, preferably imported, cut into
  ¼-inch dice

½ pound ground pork

1 tablespoon thinly sliced garlic

Pinch of crushed red pepper to taste

1 tablespoon tomato paste

1 14-ounce can of whole peeled tomatoes
Coarse or kosher salt and freshly ground black pepper to taste
1 pound *penne rigate, rigatoni,* or other short tubular pasta
¼ cup freshly grated Parmigiano, plus more for serving
Chopped fresh parsley to serve

1. In a sauté pan large enough to hold the pasta, heat the oil over medium heat and add the mortadella and ground pork. Sauté, stirring and blending until the meat is browned slightly, about 5 minutes. Add the garlic and crushed red pepper and cook for another minute. Then stir in the tomato paste. Pour the tomato liquid from the can into your pot, and then gradually crush the tomatoes, pouring more liquid into the pot as you go. Bring to a boil, immediately turn the heat to low, and simmer until the sauce has become somewhat concentrated, about 20 minutes.

2. While the sauce is cooking, bring 4 quarts of water to a boil. Salt the water, add the pasta, and cook for 2 minutes less than the recommended time on the package. Drain the pasta thoroughly and add it to sauce. Raise the heat to medium, toss the pasta to coat, about 2 minutes. Stir in the Parmigiano. Sprinkle with the chopped parsley and serve immediately, passing the grated cheese.

A Thoroughly Unorthodox Puttanesca

SERVES ROUGHLY 6 AS A FIRST COURSE
AND 4 AS A MAIN COURSE

*P*uttanesca is a dish that is described as being "in the style of the whore." If the name derives from the Italian word *puttana,* which means "whore," *puttana* in turn arises from the Latin word *putida*, which means "stinking." The sources for the name are many and varied. One is that prostitutes made this dish for the men awaiting their turn at the brothel. Another version of the story is that it was a favorite of married women who wished to limit their time in the kitchen so that they could sneak out and visit their lovers.

Returning to the sauce, there are people who find that anchovies can be overwhelming. Anchovies can also have a bit of a gritty texture to them. This also turns some people off. The ancient Greeks, and then the Romans, may have felt this way, because they came up with a solution—literally—that maintained the anchovy's vibrancy while tempering its tendency to be excruciatingly overpowering. *Garum*, or *liquamen*, was a fermented fish sauce used as a condiment in the cuisines of ancient Greece, Rome, and Byzantium. The curing process was a most odiferous one, and apt to turn one's nostrils inside out. The resulting liquid, though, was essential to Roman cookery. Italians on the Amalfi Coast are still producing this precious, albeit "stinky" brew collectively known as Colatura di Alici di Cetara. It is as pricey as it is potent, and I prefer the slightly milder anchovy-based *nuoc mam* and *nam pla* of Southeast Asia. Fish sauce evidently imparts a savory umami flavor to food and is far more palatable to most people than anchovies. I have served this dish to people who would rather gargle with Drāno than eat anchovies, and I have almost patently had positive results. The fish sauce is very salty, and you may not need to season the sauce any further. Although a true *puttanesca* would never be served with Parmigiano, my family prefers it. The choice is yours.

¼ cup extra-virgin olive oil

1½ teaspoons minced garlic

1 teaspoon crushed red pepper, or more to taste

1 28-ounce can whole peeled tomatoes

20 Liguria or Kalamata olives, pitted and thinly sliced

3 tablespoons capers, drained

2 tablespoons Thai fish sauce, or more to taste

1 pound dried Italian spaghetti

1 cup coarsely chopped fresh flat-leaf parsley

1. In a sauté pan large enough to hold the spaghetti, heat the oil over medium heat and add the garlic and crushed red pepper and cook until the garlic is just golden. Pour the tomato liquid from the can into your pot, and then gradually crush the tomatoes, pouring more liquid into the pot as you go. Bring to a boil, immediately turn the heat to low, and simmer until the sauce has become somewhat concentrated, about 20 minutes. Add the olives, capers, and fish sauce and simmer for about 5 minutes.

2. While the sauce is cooking, bring 4 quarts of water to a boil. Salt the water, add the spaghetti, and cook for 2 minutes less than the recommended time on the package. Drain the spaghetti thoroughly and add it to sauce. Raise the heat to medium, toss the pasta to coat, and cook for about 2 minutes. Stir in the parsley and serve with extra crushed red pepper and—only if you crave it—a grating of fresh Parmigiano. I said it was unorthodox.

Raw Summer Puttanesca

SERVES ROUGHLY 6 AS A FIRST COURSE
AND 4 AS A MAIN COURSE

I learned this recipe from a Neapolitan friend who swears that this is the best and only way to eat pasta puttanesca. It may seem even more unorthodox than my version, but at least it is authentically Italian. Not only is the sauce uncooked; it is actually chilled before it is poured over the pasta. Interestingly, it also has no anchovy or capers. Unlike our "lady of the evening" above, this is a sultry siren of a summer afternoon. Any pasta that will "capture" the sauce will succeed well here: conchiglie, calamari (short, wide tubes shaped like squid), or rotelle. Talk religion and politics in unfamiliar company, streak at a sporting event, or regift presents if you must, but whatever you do, do not add cheese to this dish.

> 1 pound of juicy ripe tomatoes (not paste tomatoes), seeded
>   and coarsely chopped
> 1½ teaspoons coarsely chopped garlic
> 1 teaspoon crushed red pepper, or more to taste
> 20 Liguria or Kalamata olives, pitted and coarsely chopped
> ½ cup very good extra-virgin olive oil
> Coarse or kosher salt and freshly ground pepper to taste
> 1 pound pasta (see headnote)

1. Mix all of the sauce ingredients in a bowl and refrigerate for about 2 hours.

2. Bring 4 quarts of water to a boil and add the salt. Add the pasta and cook until al dente. Drain and place in a large serving bowl. Immediately pour the sauce over the hot pasta. Toss to blend the pasta and the sauce, and serve.

Pasta with Greens and Roasted Rosemary Potatoes

SERVES ROUGHLY 6 AS A FIRST COURSE
AND 4 AS A MAIN COURSE

If the title of this recipe seems rather generic, so are the ingredients. Unlike broccoli rabe, which has its own peppery inflection, most leafy greens can be used interchangeably; and so can the pastas that accompany them. Chard, kale, and dandelion greens, among others, are all healthful ways of zipping up your pasta. I suppose that my family would have considered this a form of grazing rather than supping, but remember, my mother thought that eating the parsley garnish on your plate was laughable. Because some greens, such as kale and dandelion greens, are tougher than chard, they generally need to cook longer. Tougher greens also marry well with other substantial ingredients, as is the case in the following recipe, which includes roasted potatoes. Like a blank page or canvas, greens have so many possibilities. Similarly, choose your favorite wine with this.

1 pound small Yukon gold or new potatoes, scrubbed but not
    peeled, cut into ¼-inch pieces
1½ teaspoons coarsely chopped garlic
3 tablespoons extra-virgin olive oil
2 tablespoons coarsely chopped fresh rosemary
Coarse or kosher salt and freshly ground pepper to taste
1 pound kale (about 2 bunches)
1 tablespoon freshly squeezed lemon juice
1 pound spaghetti (or pasta of your choice)
Freshly grated Parmigiano for serving

1. Heat oven to 400 degrees.

2. Combine the potatoes, garlic, and 1 tablespoon of the olive oil on a baking sheet. Sprinkle with rosemary, salt, and pepper and toss to coat well. Spread the potatoes out in a single layer, making sure that the oil has coated the bottom of the pan. Roast the potatoes, turning them occasionally, until crisp, about 30 minutes.

3. Meanwhile, wash the kale and cut the stalks from the leaves. Cut the stalks across the grain into 1-inch pieces and set aside. Working in batches, roll the leaves like a cigar and cut into 1-inch ribbons. Keep them separate from the stalks. Heat remaining 2 tablespoons of olive oil in a large sauté pan over medium-high heat. Add the kale stalks and cook until they begin to give up some of their liquid, about 4 minutes. Add the leaves and reduce heat to low. Cover, stirring the kale occasionally, and cook until tender, 6 to 10 minutes. Transfer to a large bowl or serving dish and stir in the lemon juice.

4. Bring 4 quarts of water to a boil and add the salt. Add the pasta and cook until al dente. Drain the pasta, reserving 1/4 cup pasta water.

5. When the potatoes are done, blend with the kale, and toss with the spaghetti. Add a splash of the pasta water and toss well. Serve immediately, passing the Parmigiano.

Linguine with Broccolini in Spicy Tomato Cream Sauce

SERVES ROUGHLY 6 AS A FIRST COURSE
AND 4 AS A MAIN COURSE

Broccoli rabe, or rapini, was fairly popular among the elders of some Italian American households, but certainly not with its younger members. In one of those "I dare you moments," my sister, Donna, bet me that I could not eat two forkfuls of my grandmother's sautéed broccoli rabe. Its bitter and pungent taste caused my nose to wrinkle like the hindquarters of an African bush elephant. It figures, since broccoli rabe is actually a member of the mustard family. It is also similar to *gai lan*, bitter Chinese kale. Although I have changed my opinion about broccoli rabe, apparently others have not. This may have led the Mann Produce Company to develop a hybrid between broccoli and *gai lan*, which they called and trademarked Broccolini. In fact, that is why it is capitalized. Broccolini took off in gourmet cuisine in the 1990s and became widespread in supermarkets shortly thereafter. One wonders how we lived so long without this delectable vegetable. You can also substitute zucchini for the Broccolini, but choose broad or tubular pasta, such as *farfalle* or *penne,* to hold the sauce.

1 bunch Broccolini (about 1 pound), rough ends discarded
3 tablespoons olive oil
1½ teaspoons minced garlic
¼ teaspoon crushed red pepper, or more to taste
1 pound ripe tomatoes, seeded and chopped into ½-inch pieces
Coarse or kosher salt and freshly ground pepper to taste
½ cup heavy cream
1 pound linguine or spaghetti
A handful of fresh basil leaves, torn into ½-inch pieces
Freshly grated Parmigiano for serving

1. Bring 4 quarts of water to a boil. Salt the water and blanch the Broccolini for about 2 minutes. Remove the Broccolini with a slotted spoon or a strainer and immediately immerse in a bowl of ice water. Cut the Broccolini into 2-inch pieces and return to the cold water.

2. In a sauté pan large enough to hold the pasta, heat the oil over medium heat and add the garlic and crushed red pepper and cook until the garlic is just golden, about 2 minutes. Add the tomatoes and salt and pepper and cook, stirring, for another 5 minutes.

3. Pour in the cream and stir until it thickens slightly, about 2 minutes. Drain the reserved Broccolini and stir it into the sauce. Cook for another 2 minutes.

4. Bring 4 quarts of water to a boil and add the salt. Add the pasta and cook until al dente. Drain and toss the pasta with the sauce. Sprinkle on the basil. Serve immediately and pass the Parmigiano.

Penne with Pepper-Infused Vodka

SERVES ROUGHLY 6 AS A FIRST COURSE
AND 4 AS A MAIN COURSE

⌒◞

I may be alone in this, but I just do not get the idea of *penne* with plain vodka. I am more of a devotee of the juniper berry (gin), so the majority of vodka leaves me cold. Since most vodka is essentially neutral in flavor, and since alcohol burns off in cooking, I simply don't see the point of adding it to a sauce while cooking. Some Polish and Russian vodka, and the French Fair vodka distilled from quinoa, do have an unctuous quality and a more distinctive taste than other vodkas, but they should only be added at the end of the cooking process. Otherwise you might as well just cook with distilled water. Personally, unless you choose to use pepper-flavored vodka, I think that this dish can work just fine without vodka—not to ignore the fact that most of the time the sauce in restaurants is overcooked and has a surfeit of cream until it resembles pink library paste.

Not surprisingly, sources vary dramatically on who invented vodka sauce. On the romantic side we have Italians from Bologna and Naples credited with the recipe. On the more prosaic side you can opt for James Doty, a graduate of Columbia University. Then there is the *Williams-Sonoma Essentials of Italian* cookbook, which states that the sauce was created in the 1980s by a Roman chef for a vodka company that wanted to popularize its product in Italy. For my version I use pepper-infused vodka. You can use a brand like Stoli Hot Jalapeño or make your own pepper-infused vodka following the recipe below. Ridged *penne—penne rigate—* holds the sauce better than regular, smooth *penne lisce*. While this dish is awfully popular in restaurants, and more often than not just awful, the customary meat used is *pancetta*. I prefer hot *coppa* (also called *cappicola*, or by the infamous *Soprano*-style bastardization, *gabagoul*) for a spicier edge. As for the pasta being named *penne*, which literally translates as "pens," this is because the angled cut of the noodle sucks in the sauce, rather like the nib of a quilled pen drawing up ink from an inkwell.

3 tablespoons extra-virgin olive oil

¼ cup chopped *coppa*

½ cup chopped onion

2 teaspoons minced garlic

½ teaspoon crushed red pepper, or more to taste

1 28-ounce can of whole peeled tomatoes

Coarse or kosher salt and black pepper to taste

1 pound *penne rigate* or other ridged tubular pasta

¼ cup pepper-infused vodka (recipe follows) or best quality
   pepper vodka

½ cup heavy cream

Freshly grated Parmigiano for serving

1. In a skillet large enough to hold the pasta, heat the oil over medium heat and add the *coppa*. Sauté the *coppa* until it begins to render its fat, about 4 minutes. Stir in the onion, garlic, and crushed red pepper and continue sautéing until the vegetables have softened, about another 4 minutes. With your hands, carefully break the tomatoes apart in the can and slowly pour the juice and tomatoes into the pan and cook over medium high heat until the tomatoes come to a boil. Turn the heat to low and simmer until the tomatoes have reduced, about 15 minutes.

2. Meanwhile, bring 4 quarts of water to a boil and add the salt. Add pasta and cook until al dente.

3. Drain the pasta and add it to the tomato sauce. Toss and stir in the vodka and cream. Transfer the pasta to a large bowl. Toss again and serve immediately, passing the Parmigiano.

Pepper-Infused Vodka

Use disposable gloves when handling the chilies. And you know why!

> 1 bottle (750 L) Fair or other premium vodka
> 2 fresh red jalapeño or red Fresno peppers, slit in half length-
>   wise, stem left intact
> 2 fresh red cayenne peppers, slit in half lengthwise, stem left intact
> 1 red or orange habanero pepper, slit in half lengthwise, stem
>   left intact (optional for "hotheads")

1. Pour some of the vodka out of the bottle in order to make room for the peppers, and reserve for another use (I'm certain that you can find one). Add the peppers to the vodka. Cap it and let it stand in a cool, dark place. Test after 3 days, and let the vodka rest until it acquires the desired heat, about 1 week.

2. Remove the peppers and keep the vodka in the freezer.

A Lighter, Feisty "Alfredo"

SERVES ROUGHLY 6 AS A FIRST COURSE

AND 4 AS A MAIN COURSE

This came to me quite by accident rather than because I was looking for a lower-fat dish. I was visiting friends at their small cabin in the hinterlands of Vermont, and just as we were about to go out to dinner, I realized that it was Memorial Day. It was bucketing outside, and I thought that we should call the nearest restaurant several miles away to see if they were open. There was no answer. I decided I would cook dinner, so I perused the larder and the fridge. There was a box of fettuccine, some Parm, and a container of heavy cream. Presto! Fettuccine all'Alfredo. Or rather, presto, change-o . . . after opening up the cream and sniffing it, my nose went up like an infield fly. To say it was out of date would underestimate the amount of time that had elapsed since its demise. With the pasta water boiling, I took another peek in the fridge. There was precious little else, but there was a tub of Vermont creamy goat cheese. I had also noticed some chives growing just outside the door—a dinner was born.

I don't feel especially errant in altering this recipe, since practically every Alfredo has also strayed from the original. If Russell Belanca of Alfredo's in Rome is to be believed, the original recipe, invented around 1910 by Alfredo di Lelio for his pregnant wife, featured fresh egg pasta served only with butter and Parmigiano and no cream. The popular sauce with cream did exist later in Bologna and Florence as alla panna (with cream). In Rome it was doppio burro (double butter). How Alfredo got the credit for inventing the creamy sauce remains a mystery.

> 4 ounces of creamy goat cheese
>
> Coarse or kosher salt
>
> 1 pound of fresh egg fettuccine (homemade is preferable, but store-bought or dried egg fettuccine or *tagliatelle* will do in a pinch)
>
> ½ cup freshly grated Parmigiano, plus more for serving
>
> Freshly ground black pepper to taste
>
> A pinch freshly ground nutmeg
>
> 2 tablespoons finely chopped chives

1. Bring 4 quarts of water to a boil. Meanwhile, spread the goat cheese in a large, wide bowl.

2. When the water is boiling, add salt and then add the pasta and cook until al dente. Just before the pasta is done, take about 2 tablespoons of the pasta water and stir it into the goat cheese. Drain the pasta, reserving 1/4 cup pasta water.

3. Add the pasta to the bowl and stir briefly. Blend in the Parmigiano, pepper, and nutmeg. Add just enough of the reserved pasta water to enhance the creaminess. Sprinkle the chives over the pasta and serve immediately with additional Parmigiano.

Calamari with Mushrooms

SERVES ROUGHLY 6 AS A FIRST COURSE

AND 4 AS A MAIN COURSE

For anyone who cannot live without mushrooms or pasta, this dish is for you. This recipe came to me when I was working for Lisa Ekus Public Relations. We were taking on a client from Japan who was about to distribute *maitake* mushrooms in this country. He brought us a basketful, and he wanted us to try them. He warned us that they could not be eaten raw because they produced hallucinations. They must be cooked, and I offered to try them out. (By the way, they aren't hallucinogenic, I can tell you, because the first thing I did with them before cooking them was to try a couple of bites.) *Maitakes*, cousin of hen of the woods, grow in clusters and are easily torn into shreds. In Italy they are commonly known as the *signorina* mushrooms. No, I don't know why. Not being able to find *maitakes* of my own at the time, I took large cremini mushrooms and grated them through the large holes on my Cuisinart grating disk. *Maitakes* are not as difficult to find anymore, but they are expensive compared to cremini mushrooms. So the latter is a serviceable alternative. On a scientific note, in 2009, a phase I/II human trial, conducted by Memorial Sloan Kettering Cancer Center, showed that *maitake* mushrooms could stimulate the immune systems of breast cancer patients.

If you are wondering about the *calamari* in this recipe, it is not the squid but short tubular pasta that resembles the cut-up sea creature.

If you cannot find *calamari*, any wide pasta, such as *rigatoni*, will do. I have apologized for my use of truffle oil elsewhere, and I feel further atonement is not necessary.

2 tablespoons unsalted butter

2 tablespoons extra-virgin olive oil

½ pound *maitake*, hen of the woods, bottom trimmed,
   or 1 pound large cremini mushrooms coarsely grated

1½ teaspoons chopped garlic

½ teaspoon crushed red pepper, or more to taste

¼ cup dry white wine

1 cup chicken or vegetable stock

2 tablespoons coarsely chopped fresh flat-leaf parsley

1 pound *calamari*, *paccheri*, or other wide, round tubular pasta

Dash of good-quality truffle oil

Parmigiano for serving

Freshly ground pepper to taste

1. Place the butter and the oil over medium heat in a large skillet that will hold all the pasta. While the butter is melting, break the *maitakes* into small shreds and stir them into the skillet to coat. Add the garlic and hot pepper and cook until the mushrooms give up their moisture, 8 to 10 minutes. If you are using the grated cremini mushrooms, follow the same cooking procedure.

2. Meanwhile, bring 4 quarts of water to a boil.

3. Just before the mushrooms are about to stick to the pan, add the white wine and cook until it has nearly evaporated. Add the chicken stock and continue cooking until it is reduced by one-third, about 10 minutes. Stir in the parsley.

4. When the water is boiling, add the salt and the pasta and cook until al dente. Drain the pasta, reserving 1/4 cup of the pasta water. Toss the pasta with the sauce in the skillet and add the truffle oil. Continue cooking until the pasta is well coated. Add some of the reserved pasta water if the sauce has cooked down too much. Serve immediately, passing the Parmigiano and freshly ground pepper.

Paccheri with Ricotta and Tomatoes

SERVES ROUGHLY 6 AS A FIRST COURSE AND 4 AS A MAIN COURSE

If you took your garden hose and cut it into sections several inches long, you would have something that looks like *paccheri*—and a fairly useless garden hose. Unlike *rigatoni*, which are ridged, *paccheri* are smooth and will flatten when they are cooked. The name is said to be rooted in the Neapolitan dialect *paccaria* for "slap." Don't ask why, because nobody knows. Perhaps that's why someone decided to invent a story to make the pasta all the more romantic. The purported belief is that the word *pacchero* comes from a now-lost word for "squid," because the round tube resembled *calamari*. Nobody is betting much on this, however. The more fascinating history of this tubular pasta was that it was invented as a way to smuggle Italian garlic into Prussia, or present-day Austria. The Prussian government banned trade in Italian garlic in the 1600s because it was far superior to their own. So, it is said, Italian garlic farmers hid cloves of garlic inside *paccheri* when crossing the border. The ruse was never discovered, and the Prussian garlic industry collapsed as a result. If you don't believe that, then trust me that *paccheri* are good eating, especially as an *arrabbiata*, with a mushroom sauce, a *ragù*, or in the popular, quick Neapolitan dish that follows. Oh, it also goes well with squid and garlic.

1 pound *paccheri*

2 cups or so of Spicy Raw Tomato Sauce with Garlic and Basil (page 57), or light tomato sauce of your choice

1 cup crumbled fresh sheep's milk ricotta

½ cup freshly grated Parmigiano, plus more for serving

Coarse or kosher salt and freshly ground pepper to taste
½ cup freshly torn basil leaves

1. Bring 4 quarts of water to a boil and add salt. Add the pasta and cook until al dente. Drain the pasta, reserving 1/4 cup pasta water.

2. While the pasta is cooking, bring the tomato sauce to a gentle simmer in a pan large enough to hold the pasta. Add the cheeses and salt and pepper, stir to blend, and turn off heat.

3. Drain the pasta and add it to the sauce. Stir until well coated and add pasta water if needed. Transfer to a serving bowl, if you like, and serve immediately. Top individual plates with extra Parmigiano, basil, and more pepper if desired.

Baked Penne with Mushrooms

SERVES ROUGHLY 6 AS A FIRST COURSE
AND 4 AS A MAIN COURSE

lthough we never had baked *ziti* at home, I don't think that I ever suffered from a lack of it growing up. Whether visiting neighbors or eating at friends' houses, there was inevitably a pan of baked *ziti* smothered in mozzarella to feed the masses. I would always try to get some of the brown, crisp cheese that clung to the edges of the pan. I am still a fiend for the crispy cheese that clings to the baked pasta, but that cheese is now Fontina. Fontina is an Italian cow's milk cheese that originally hails from the Aosta Valley in the Alps. The cheese may have been produced in Italy since the twelfth century, but it was never a guest in our house.

Although Italian Fontina is available in cheese shops and specialty stores, the Swedish and Danish versions are more commonly found in American markets. They can be distinguished from Italian Fontina by their red wax rinds. Italian Fontina has a natural brownish rind due to aging. It is also firmer and packs more of a bite than its foreign imitators. Since it is also ideal for melting, Italians use it in soups, fondues, and almost anything that comes from the oven. Its nutty, earthy flavor wins hands down over mozzarella. Sally Schneider in her exceptional *A New Way to Cook* offers a milder rendition of the following dish by using *ricotta salata*. This is a very hearty pasta dish, and it calls for serving of red wine over white.

> 2 ounces dried porcini mushrooms
> 2 tablespoons extra-virgin olive oil
> 1 cup coarsely chopped onions
> 1½ teaspoons finely chopped garlic
> 1 teaspoon crushed red pepper, or more to taste
> 1 pound cremini mushrooms, thinly sliced
> ½ cup dry white wine
> 1 tablespoon finely chopped fresh oregano leaves
> 1 28-ounce can whole peeled tomatoes
> Coarse or kosher salt and freshly ground pepper to taste
> 1 pound smooth *penne*
> ½ cup freshly grated Parmigiano, plus more for serving
> ½ pound Fontina, coarsely grated, mixed with ½ cup freshly
>   grated Parmigiano

1. Place the porcini mushrooms in a bowl and cover with boiling water. Let the mushrooms soak for 30 minutes. Strain mixture through a fine-mesh sieve or cheesecloth, saving the mushroom water. Rinse mushrooms until they are completely free of any grit, and coarsely chop them.

2. Heat a 2-quart wide saucepan over medium heat. Add 1 tablespoon of the olive oil and sauté onions until soft, about 4 minutes. Add the garlic and crushed red pepper and cook for another 3 or 4 minutes, or until the vegetables begin to turn a golden brown.

3. Stir in half the mushroom liquid, scraping the pan as you go. Add the wine and oregano and bring to a boil. Stir in all of the mushrooms. Start pouring the tomato liquid into your pan and quickly crush the tomatoes by hand and add them to the sauce. Add the salt and pepper. Turn heat to low and simmer until sauce begins to thicken, about 20 minutes.

4. Preheat the oven to 375 degrees.

5. Meanwhile, bring 4 quarts of water to a boil and add the salt. Add the pasta and cook for about 3 minutes less than the recommended time. Drain the pasta and return it to its pot along with the mushroom sauce. Toss the *penne* with the sauce and blend in the ½ cup of Parmigiano. Coat the bottom and sides of a wide baking dish with the other tablespoon of olive oil. Pour the *penne* into the baking dish, spreading the penne and sauce to uniformly fill the dish.

6. Sprinkle the Fontina-Parmigiano mixture evenly all over the pasta. Set the dish on the middle rack of the oven and bake for 20 to 25 minutes, or until the cheese topping is crusty and deep golden brown and the sauce is bubbling up at the edges. Serve, passing the extra Parmigiano.

Homemade Pasta Dough

SERVES ROUGHLY 4

Ahand-cranked pasta machine is just fine for the occasional pasta dough, particularly if you have a dutiful assistant to help with the extrusion of the dough. If, however, you plan to take the endeavor on in earnest, I would recommend a machine with a motor. This will free up your extra hand and help you work at an even pace.

> 2½ cups durum semolina pasta flour, plus extra flour as needed to prevent sticking
> 3 extra-large fresh eggs at room temperature

1. On a wooden or other smooth, warm surface, make a well of the flour and crack the eggs into it. Beat the eggs gently with a fork, and gradually pull the flour from the walls into the center, carefully incorporating the flour until it comes together.

2. Quickly, using both hands, knead the mixture into a ball. Knead well until the dough is moist and firm but not sticky. Form a ball, wrap it tightly with plastic wrap, and let it rest for about 20 minutes.

3. Cut dough into 4 quarters and cover each with a cloth to prevent drying. Set your pasta machine to wide and pass the first quarter through twice. If you sense that the dough is too sticky, lightly flour the rollers. Reduce the rollers a notch at a time and continue as above, rolling through twice, until the dough has passed through the thinnest rollers. Lay the dough on clean, dry towels or parchment paper and continue with the other pieces of dough. Allow to dry for up to 1 hour until leathery. This may take longer depending on the humidity.

4. Most machines come with cutters for *linguine* to *tagliatelle*, but *pappardelle* is always cut by hand. For *pappardelle*, using a pasta or pizza cutter, slice dough lengthwise at ½-inch intervals. As with all of the cut pastas, roll them around your hand to make nests and set them aside on parchment paper until ready to cook.

Timpano

SERVES MANY

It is hard to imagine that anyone reading this book has not seen the classic Italian food film *Big Night.* It boasts a stellar cast, but the true star is the glorious *timpano.* Named for the Italian word for "drum"—also called *timballo*—this extravagant fantasy is the stuff, and stuffing, that dreams are made of. If a costume department makes a typical screen star shine, the food stylist is the magician who embellishes this delectable counterpart. In the case of *Big Night,* it was New York food stylist Deb DiSabatino. She, along with many other stylists of the period, was in the vanguard of what we now impishly call "food porn." With Facebook and Pinterest, among other sites, food porn is everywhere. And, like its sexual alter ego, it is predominantly a spectator's affair. Well, here is your chance to get in on the action. Originally a prized dish served at feasts in Emilia-Romagna, the *timpano* has many variations—with each cook trying to outdo another. Since first seeing *Big Night,* I have pored over many recipes, and I have attempted the *timpano* several times. The recipe that follows is the result of those efforts. I cannot overestimate the praise you will receive upon presenting this dish at your next feast.

Of course you will need an appropriate "drum" to beat out your praises. In *Big Night* they used a large enamel wash pan, which, like everything else under the sun, you can find on eBay. I purchased my pasta drum online from FGpizza.com. It is a thing of beauty and can also double as a decorative serving bowl. Otherwise, a 4-quart oven-proof metal mixing bowl will work. (On a note of personal taste, I omit the hard-boiled eggs, and I have therefore listed them as optional.)

FOR THE PASTA FROLLA:

3 cups all-purpose flour

½ teaspoon coarse or kosher salt

3 extra-large fresh eggs at room temperature, lightly beaten

1 tablespoon extra-virgin olive oil

¼ cup cold water, as needed

Olive oil to grease the pan

FOR THE FILLING:

1 pound cooked *penne* or other short tubular pasta, very
al dente (about 2 minutes less than directed)

5 cups *ragù* (page 137) or your favorite sauce, at room
temperature

3 tablespoons extra-virgin olive oil

1 cup sharp provolone, cut into ¼-inch cubes

1 cup Genoa salami, cut into ¼-inch cubes

1 cup mortadella, cut into ¼-inch cubes

1 dozen cooked meatballs (page 178), at room temperature

6 hard-boiled eggs, shelled and quartered (optional)

⅓ cup freshly grated Pecorino Romano

Freshly grated Parmigiano, for serving

TO MAKE THE PASTA FROLLA:

Mix the flour and salt together in a bowl and add the eggs and olive oil. Stir until the dough forms a ball, adding water as needed. Set out on a floured work surface and knead until smooth, about 5 minutes. Tightly wrap in plastic and set aside for about an hour.

FOR THE TIMPANO:

1. Preheat the oven to 350 degrees. Toss the cooked *penne* with 2 cups of the *ragù*. Grease the pan or bowl with 2 tablespoons of the olive oil. Roll out the pasta on a floured surface until it is about ⅛ inch thick and about 26 inches in diameter (or just wide enough that it will

line a 4-quart bowl with enough of an overlap so that the dough will completely cover the filling). Carefully line the bowl with the dough, draping the extra dough over the sides.

2. Distribute one-third of the pasta with sauce over the pasta-lined bowl. Top with ½ cup of the *ragù* and then half the provolone, salami, and mortadella. Add half of the meatballs, half of the eggs (if you're using them), and half the Pecorino Romano. Pour about 1½ cups of the *ragù* over that.

3. Add another one-third of the pasta. Top with the remaining provolone, salami, mortadella, meatballs, eggs (if you're using them), and Pecorino Romano. Spread on the remaining *ragù*.

4. Fold the pasta dough over the filling to seal completely. Trim away and discard any double layers of dough. Brush the pasta with the remaining 1 tablespoon of oil. Bake until lightly browned, about 45 minutes to an hour. The *timpano* is done when the internal temperature is about 120 degrees. Remove from the oven and let stand for at least 10 minutes. Using a knife or pastry spatula, loosen the pasta around the base of the *timpano* and tap the bowl with your knuckles. Place a serving platter over the bowl and carefully turn it upside down. Let the *timpano* rest for another 10 minutes. Slice as you would a cake, and pass the grated Parmigiano.

Mostly Meat

Red meat is not bad for you.
Now blue-green meat, that's bad for you!
—TOMMY SMOTHERS

The only meat dishes we were served in my home that were remotely Italian were spaghetti and meatballs, or maybe spaghetti and sausage. I do not count the ground meat in the lasagne, as it was overwhelmed by buckets of pasty ricotta and pounds of gooey mozzarella. If you wish to consider meatloaf in a puddle of tomato sauce Italian, I did not even consider my mother's meatloaf a loaf. Graced with three old-time butchers on the same block around the corner, we did have the opportunity to eat freshly butchered meat, which is now a rarity in most cities. If she had only known how to cook it!

The status quo was to let a roast cook into overwhelmingly overdoneness. She still prefers it that way. Unwittingly, however, my mother set me on the path to become a true carnivore. Whether she was in a rush that day or just forgetful of the time, a roast that emerged from the oven one Sunday was a rosy pink. That single roast changed my mind about beef. I asked that she repeat her error at every chance. From the thinly sliced minute steaks to the special once-a-month Sunday roast, the beef was rare. And rare indeed, as no one expected a twelve-year-old who was something of a dork to tell his mother how to cook. But I was number one son, and she attempted to accommodate me (read, shut me up). She would cook the meat rare, slice a couple of pieces for me, and then throw it back in the oven to be properly ruined. USDA aside, I still maintain that there are two types of people who don't eat meat: vegetarians and people who eat meat well-done.

The sight of juices flowing from my portions of the roast absolutely appalled my sister. I proffered a forkful of the crimson-tinted beef to her, telling her how good it was, but Donna would have nothing to do with it. So could it be my fault then that my sister is a vegetarian? I try to take no blame for my own misdeeds and, therefore, skirt the issue of why she has such a moral issue with eating dead flesh, but Donna did not take to sharing my revelation. In my defense, there was also the matter of the lunchbox ham sandwich prepared by

The real reason my sister became a vegetarian?

my mother for Donna one day. Recalling Sherlock Holmes's discretion in the story concerning the giant rat of Sumatra, Donna's story is one for which the world is not yet prepared. After many years of struggling with her conscience, my sister did march forth into the army of vegetarians and has maintained a strict vegetarian regimen ever since. Moreover she is sincere about it. Over the years I have met strayed vegetarians, and even dutiful vegetarians, who admitted that during their prolonged years of grazing they occasionally craved a great cheeseburger. She does not. As I see it, that is a true appreciation of her choice. For me, the idea of expunging a burger from my diet is as crazy as the ruminations of a headless chicken.

As a further defense, the burger has been good to me. In the summer of 1991 Valdina, my son Tristan, and I were planning to pull up very different stakes and move from our temporary home in Buenos Aires to Paris. On the day I learned that this would not come to pass, I drove down to a local supermarket to restock the wine cellar—albeit meagerly. While there, I spotted a contest brochure for the Sutter Home Build a Better Burger competition. Having spent three years traveling back and forth to Argentina, I had become quite accustomed to their renowned beef. Unlike today, when one is able to find excellent naturally raised grass-fed beef, Western Massachusetts was sorely lacking that option twenty-five years ago. I had experimented with mixtures of ingredients, including lamb and beef, and I sent in a recipe. Although the prize-winning burger is not by any measure Italian, I have included it here.

Okay, So These Are Not Italian Burgers

SERVES 6

W hen I entered the Sutter Home Build a Better Burger contest, naturally I did not have the faintest thought that I might be flown out to the Napa Valley to compete with eleven others for a chance to win the grand prize of $10,000, but there were local prizes of $100, and since I thought I might have a shot at that, I sent in a recipe. The rest is history, as they say, and I still have the oversized replica check in my basement.

"The most happy fella in the whole Napa Valley."

CILANTRO-MINT CHUTNEY
⅓ cup plain yogurt

2 tablespoons chopped
  onion

1½ fresh jalapeño chilies,
  seeded and chopped

1½ tablespoons peeled,
  chopped fresh ginger

⅓ cup fresh mint leaves

¾ cup cilantro leaves

1 teaspoon finely chopped garlic

½ teaspoon coarse or kosher salt

Pinch of sugar

PATTIES

1 pound lean ground lamb

1 pound ground sirloin

1½ teaspoons finely chopped garlic

½ cup crumbled feta cheese

⅓ cup pitted and finely minced Kalamata olives

1 teaspoon coarse or kosher salt

¼ cup extra-virgin olive oil

1 teaspoon ground cumin mixed with 1 teaspoon ground
   coriander

Olive oil, for brushing on the grill rack

6 thick pita breads (such as Father Sam's, available online)

6 thick tomato slices

6 thin red onion slices

6 red leaf lettuce leaves

1. To make the chutney, combine all of the ingredients in a blender or food processor and blend thoroughly. Cover and refrigerate until ready to serve.

2. Prepare a medium-hot fire of natural hardwood charcoal in a grill with a cover, or preheat a gas grill to medium-high.

3. To make the patties, combine the lamb, ground sirloin, garlic, cheese, olives, and salt in a large bowl. Handling the meat as little as possible to avoid compacting it, mix well. Divide the mixture into 6 equal portions and form the portions into patties that will fit the pita breads. Brush the patties with the ¼ cup olive oil, and then sprinkle with the spice mixture.

4. When the grill is ready, brush the grill rack with olive oil. Place the patties on the rack, cover, and cook, turning once, until done to preference, about 4 minutes on each side for rare (120 to 125 degrees). During the last few minutes of grilling, place the pita breads on the outer edges of the grill rack and toast lightly.

5. To assemble the burgers, slice open just enough of the pita bread to fit the ingredients, and carefully spread the bread apart to form a pocket. Stuff a patty into each pocket and spoon an equal portion of the chutney over each patty. Add a tomato slice, an onion slice, and a lettuce leaf in each pocket and serve.

Mostly Meat
(continued)

It should go without saying, but I will say it here: Let the meat come to room temperature before cooking. Meat right from the fridge may be too cold inside to cook evenly. The outside can have a nice char, but the inside may be undercooked. As to telling when a steak is done, there are several ways to gauge this. The most common one (and pretty unreliable if you ask me) is by comparing it to the flesh between your thumb and forefinger: The pliable flesh of an open hand is said to be comparable to the touch of a rare steak, and the tight flesh of a closed fist would be well-done. This would be just peachy if we all had the same types of hands, but we don't.

Most cookbooks do not bother to give you internal temperatures for meat, assuming that if you follow their recommended time, your steak will come out perfectly. Since fires vary from grill to grill, you could be ruining an excellent cut of meat by overcooking it. Unless you are comfortable with calculating doneness, I would suggest using an instant-read thermometer. I unapologetically use one all the time. The USDA and I have parted company regarding the doneness of meat, but that is no reason for you to do so if you are wary of food-borne illness. The USDA recommendation for beef, pork, and lamb is at least 145 degrees. I tend to err on the side of flavor rather than caution. Bear in mind that your meat will still cook after being removed from the grill. If you prefer your meat cooked according to your preference, these temperatures can serve as a guideline: Before resting your meat after cooking, 120–125 degrees will produce a rare steak; 125–130 degrees for medium rare; and 130–135 degrees for medium. After that, you are on your own.

Meatballs

(APPROXIMATELY 25 TO 30)

"The meatball is a food with 'permanent culinary refugee status' stamped on its passport," or so says John Thorne in *Outlaw Cook*. I think we all know by now that spaghetti with meatballs is strictly American fare, and that dynamic duo on a plate is scorned as an aberration by many Italians. But despite how much some critics may rail against meatballs as not even being Italian, Italians, and especially southern Italians, do enjoy their *polpette*. Pellegrino Artusi pretty much summed it up in his 1891 *La scienza in cucina e l'arte di mangiar bene* (*The Science of Cooking and the Art of Eating Well*): "Do not think for a moment that I would be so pretentious as to tell you how to make meatballs. This is a dish that everyone knows how to make. . . ." As you might suspect, he did not associate meatballs with spaghetti. They were a course in themselves served with garlic, parsley, lemon, and an egg sauce. Artusi molded them into the size of eggs.

Today in Italy they tend to be somewhat smaller than what you find in restaurants here. Be that as it may, they are always served as a main course or in soup, and usually without tomato sauce. In the Abruzzo region of Italy, especially in the province of Teramo, the meatballs are typically the size of marbles, and are called *polpettine*. Small oval meatballs of ground pork, veal, and beef, christened *cvapcici* (pronounced *ch'vahp-chee-chee*) are popular in Trieste. Grilled rather than fried, they are generally served with a purée of roasted sweet peppers, onion, and vinegar. It would appear that if Italians did not eat meatballs, they would probably be one of the few peoples on earth who do not.

That said, everybody I know loves meatballs. It was only fairly recently, however, that our "foodie" friends mentioned that guilty pleasure above a whisper. Between retro-chic and nostalgia for comfort food, meatballs are back in fashion. In New York City alone at least a dozen restaurants specializing in meatballs have opened. The Meatball Shop, with four locations in New York, anchors its entire menu on its meatballs. If you are not interested in a daily special of Mediterranean Lamb Balls with Raisins, Walnuts and Mint, you can make up your own entree by choosing from their different varieties and sauces. You can even determine how you'd like your balls served.

In the past, personal recipes for meatballs were the revered province and pride of every Italian American grandmother. Moreover, those little old ladies irreverently looked down on anyone else's meatballs with derision or jealous scorn. Even Nanny spoke derisively of her own sister's meatballs. They had nothing to fear from my mother's meatballs. It is true that they were balls in the broadest sense of the definition, but "meateorites" would more aptly describe their misshapen appearance. To compare them to snowflakes would do a great injustice to snowflakes. And yet, like the snowflake, each and every one was a singular shape unto itself. Over the years people have asked me for my recipe for meatballs. I have never given it out. This was not because I was a Grinch or prone to secrecy (as this book attests just the opposite). I simply did not have one. Every time that I made meatballs it was as if my hand was guided by the Paraclete and followed his bidding. Here, I hope, is more or less what I do. The traditional triumvirate of meatballs is beef, veal, and pork, but I think the lamb gives it a richer tone than beef.

But I am not the only one to experiment here, as the Carving Board in Los Angeles demonstrated with their "Spaghetti Meatball-wich." They describe it thus: "Sliced beef meatballs topped with a garlic basil marinara and mozzarella cheese, served between Parmesan spaghetti bread." While they do not divulge the name of the mad scientist who created this, you can almost bet that it will be served by someone named Igor.

One final note about preparing meatballs: It is better to sauté the onions first, as raw onion imparts a sharper taste and can often cause the meat not to adhere properly. To end with a quote by Thorne from 1992, "Meatballs are a dish of the aspiring poor and the displaced genteel—and especially, the food of artists, students, dreamers, and other malcontents who have taught themselves to wear their poverty with a flourish." But, like the artists, students, dreamers, and malcontents, meatballs have traded in their tattered threads for a cloak of respectability.

> 1 tablespoon olive or canola oil
> ¾ cup chopped onion
> 1 cup dry breadcrumbs or *panko* (or more if the mixture is too moist)
> 1½ tablespoons finely chopped garlic
> 3 tablespoons chopped parsley
> 1 teaspoon crumbled dried tarragon
> ½ cup freshly grated Pecorino Romano
> ½ cup Parmigiano
> Pinch of freshly grated nutmeg
> Coarse or kosher salt and freshly ground pepper to taste
> 1 pound ground lamb
> 1 pound ground pork
> 2 eggs, beaten
> 1 quart Long-Simmered Summer Tomato Sauce, heated, plus ½ cup at room temperature (page 59)
> Flour for dusting
> ½ cup canola, vegetable, or other high-smoke-point oil, with more as needed

1. Heat the oil over medium heat and sauté onion in a large skillet until just soft, or as they say in the restaurant world, until they sweat. Set aside to cool briefly while gathering up the rest of your ingredients. Combine everything, including the onions, through the salt and pepper and blend well. Add the meat, eggs, and room-temperature sauce, and knead until the ingredients are fully incorporated. The mixture should be only slightly sticky to the touch.

2. Dust a large baking sheet with flour. Wetting your hands so the meat mixture does not stick, scoop enough meat to form 1-inch balls. Roll them in the flour to lightly coat them. You should have about 30 meatballs.

3. Keep the remaining tomato sauce on a simmer.

4. In a large nonstick skillet, heat half the oil on high. When the oil begins to ripple, add the meatballs in batches, not crowding them. Let them cook until brown on the bottom, and then turn them gradually until all of the meatballs have browned all over. Add them to the sauce and continue with the rest of the meatballs, adding more oil as necessary. Simmer the meatballs in the sauce for another 15 minutes and taste for seasonings.

Note: You may store them in batches, or serve them immediately, but let them rest in sauce in the fridge overnight for the gioia di polpette—"the joy of meatballs," if I may say so myself.

Florentine Grilled Steak (Bistecca alla Fiorentina)

SERVES 2 WITH LEFTOVERS (MAYBE)

I don't know what my father would have thought of this steak, as it does not have the character of a petroleum by-product. Finding the right beef for a true *Bistecca alla Fiorentina* in the United States may not be as difficult as locating Komodo dragon cutlets, but not by much. Not only is the meat served rare; the beef itself is rare. Even the Italians are hard-pressed to find the meat of the revered Chianina cattle, the huge white oxen raised in the Val di Chiana, near Arezzo. The Chianina (pronounced *kee-a-nee-na*) may well be one of the oldest breeds of cattle in existence. They were praised by the Georgic poets Columella and Virgil and were the models for Roman sculptures. Chianina beef costs at least $30 a pound, which is about a third more than Italian prime beef. The meat is of such a superior quality that according to one cook quoted in Steven Raichlen's *Bar-*

becue! Bible, "When you eat fiorentina, fiorentina is all you eat. The only suitable vegetable is wine." I'll eat and drink to that.

Chianina beef is so tender and flavorful that it is quickly cooked over the very high heat of a wood fire and then seasoned only *after* the steak is done. After cooking about 6 minutes per side, the steak is topped with salt, pepper, and copious amounts of rich extra-virgin olive oil, and allowed to rest for about 5 minutes. Unless you have access to the finest dry-aged beef and a wood fire, it may be better to follow Bruce Aidells's advice and quick- and slow-cook the beef. Since the traditional method of grilling, as described above, is self-explanatory, I will describe the other method below. Ada Boni explains that "a Florentine steak is at least 1-inch thick, cut from the rib of a younger steer, and well hung." I'll let you take it from there.

Having spent a bundle already, you might as well break the bank and serve your steak with a fine bottle of Brunello di Montalcino.

½ cup best quality extra-virgin olive oil
Coarse or kosher salt and freshly ground pepper to taste
1½- to 2-inch-thick porterhouse steak (about 2 pounds),
    dry-aged
Handful of hickory or apple chips, soaked for about an hour
Lemon wedges
Shaved fresh Parmigiano-Reggiano (optional)

1. If you are not following the traditional method described above, let the steak come to room temperature and marinate it in ¼ cup of the olive oil and salt and pepper for at least an hour. Turn occasionally.

2. Light a hardwood charcoal fire on one side of your grill, or heat half of your gas grill. When the fire is very hot, grill each side of the steak over the charcoal side for about 3 minutes per side. Transfer the steak to the other side of the grill. Lift the grate and add the hickory chips to the hot side of the grill. Cover the grill and turn the steak every 2 minutes until the internal temperature reaches 115 degrees for very rare, or to your preference. After removing the steak, tent loosely with aluminum foil, remembering that the steak will continue cooking while it rests.

3. Remove the steak to a platter that will catch all of the juices. Top the steak with more salt and pepper and drizzle with the remaining ¼ cup of olive oil. Let the steak rest for about 5 minutes. Carve the steak into ½-inch slices. Pour the juices over the steak and serve with the lemon slices and the Parmigiano, if desired.

Sliced Steak, Tomato, Arugula, and Parmigiano (Tagliata alla Fiorentina)

SERVES 4 TO 6

If *Bistecca alla Fiorentina* is the flashy Lamborghini of steaks, *Tagliata alla Fiorentina* is the reliable little compact Italian Casalini. And like the Casalini, it is little known outside of Italy, but that is changing—for the steak, anyway. Modeled on the *bistecca*, *tagliata* is humbly salted and traditionally grilled. Using other cuts of beef from other cattle, *tagliata* is homey fare that forgoes the pomp and ceremony, as well as the price tag. The method of cooking is also not as stringent. Essentially *a tagliata* is a name for the method of serving rather than cooking. The word *tagliata* comes from the verb *tagliare*, meaning "to cut or to slice." (In fact, a cutting board in Italian is *tagliere*.) Given that much leeway, the steak can also be pan-fried. And that is how I like to prepare it. That is also the way my mother occasionally prepared her round steak—with some success.

My favorite cut for this is the hanger steak—a cut that was unknown to the public until very recently. The steak is cut from the "hanging" diaphragm of a steer, and there is only one per animal. It was also called "butcher's steak" because butchers would often keep this flavorful steak for themselves rather than offer it for sale. You could substitute flank steak, but hanger steak is about one-third the price. Another inexpensive cut is the flat iron steak. Both the hanger and the flat iron steak, once hard to find, are now appearing at finer markets and food co-ops. Similarly, both cuts have little fat and must be served rare to medium-rare or they will be tough.

1½ teaspoons finely chopped garlic
2 tablespoons coarsely chopped fresh rosemary
½ teaspoon crushed red pepper, or more to taste
Coarse or kosher salt and plenty of very coarsely cracked
    pepper
2 teaspoons extra-virgin olive oil for marinating, plus another
    tablespoon for cooking
2 hanger steaks (or flat iron), about 2 pounds
8 cups arugula or watercress (about 6 ounces)
2 large tomatoes cut into ¼-inch slices
¼ cup thinly sliced shallots
1 lemon, cut into wedges
Tradizionale di Modena balsamic vinegar (optional)
Pecorino Romano or Parmigiano, for shaving

1. Mix the garlic, rosemary, crushed red pepper, and salt and black pepper with 2 teaspoons of olive oil. Pat steaks dry and coat them with the mixture. Let stand at room temperature for about an hour, or refrigerate for longer.

2. Place a cast-iron skillet over high heat and let the pan really heat up, about 5 minutes (and turn on your exhaust fan if you have one!). Add the remaining tablespoon of oil to the skillet. Swirl the oil quickly and immediately add the steaks. Cook, turning the steaks until they are completely crusted and browned, 8 to 10 minutes (or until the internal temperature reads 120 to 125 degrees for rare).

3. Transfer the steaks to a cutting board and let them rest for 5 to 10 minutes. Meanwhile spread the arugula on a platter. Top with the tomatoes and shallots and place the lemon wedges around the edges.

Thinly slice the steaks on the bias against the grain and arrange on top of the salad. Drizzle with more olive oil (and the balsamic vinegar if desired). Liberally shave the cheese over the steak and serve.

Definitely Not My Mom's Steak Pizzaiola

SERVES 4

S he called it steak *Pizzaiola,* but as Italian food, that's about as far as it went—or ran screaming into the night. Round steak does not have much marbling and can dry out if not cooked properly. My mother went the extra mile here and gave Benjamin Goodrich a ride for his money. It was a meal that my mother thought she could cook, and she would serve it once a week. Eventually my otherwise stoic father asked her to stop making this horrific combination of cubed round steak and brown water. He confided to me that it was like eating rubber bathed in a street puddle. This is not being fair to "brown," which is indeed a color. The complexion of our mess would make a UPS truck appear like a young multicolored coifed David Bowie on tour in Hamburg by comparison.

My sister, Donna, also remembers our father not eating much at dinner and telling our mother that he wasn't that hungry because he had been to a large business lunch. Steak Pizzaiola is a classic Neapolitan dish, and the meat is sometimes pounded to tenderize it. It is then cooked in a spicy tomato sauce. As the sauce resembles the sauce used to make pizza, it was named *pizzaiola,* or "pizza style." Although round steak was my mother's steak of choice, I prefer skirt steak or flat iron steak. Our debacle was served with Minute Rice. Granted, Minute Rice may have advanced leagues since the stuff of my youth, but I wouldn't know. Instead, I would recommend a broad egg noodle for a stroganoff-style meal.

2 tablespoons extra-virgin olive oil

2 skirt steaks, about 2 pounds, patted dry

1½ teaspoons finely chopped garlic

2 cups thinly sliced red and green bell pepper

½ teaspoon crushed red pepper, or more to taste

½ teaspoon dried oregano

1 cup fresh or canned diced tomatoes (Muir Glen Fire Roasted tomatoes are superb here)

Coarse or kosher salt and freshly ground pepper to taste

A handful of fresh basil leaves, torn into ½-inch pieces

Cooked broad egg noodles (optional)

1. Heat the oil in a large skillet over medium-high heat. Add the beef and quickly brown on both sides, 2 to 3 minutes.

2. Set the meat aside and leave just enough fat to coat the bottom of the skillet. Add the garlic and peppers and sauté over medium heat until soft, about 4 minutes. Add the crushed red pepper, oregano, tomatoes, and salt and pepper. Lower the heat and simmer for about 10 minutes to allow the tomatoes to give off some of their liquid and the peppers to soften further.

3. Return the meat to the pan and cook for another 5 minutes or so until warmed through. Transfer the steak to a cutting board and let rest for about 5 minutes while the sauce continues to simmer. Thinly slice the steak against the grain and ladle the sauce over it. Serve immediately, topped with the fresh basil over a platter of noodles, if you so desire.

ℳeatloaf with
Wild ℳushrooms

SERVES 6 (WITH, HOPEFULLY, LEFTOVERS)

When my mother was feeling diabolically creative, she would attempt an "Italian" meatloaf. If you wish to consider a clump of ground beef, steeped in a swamp of tomato sauce Italian, a loaf, more power to you. With the consistency of garden compost, the agglomeration that was ladled out of a Bundt pan onto a plate was more of a Sloppy Giuseppe. Where she got the idea of making this round, lumpish Hula-Hoop is far beyond me. There was another ingredient that set this dish well apart from other Italian-style meatloaves. I could be wrong, but I think it was Heinz ketchup. On one occasion she served it with canned green beans in the center, inspired by a Del Monte Green Beans ad in a magazine. Thanks to the Internet, I was able to find a copy of the very same recipe. It went by the enticing name Green Bean Pizzarino and was touted as "Glorified Meat Loaf with Tender-Crisp Del Monte Green Beans." I wonder if the creator was ever let out of confinement.

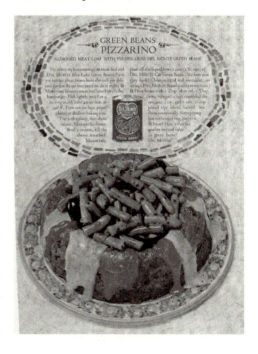

When making the following recipe, know that it is going to be rather loose when you're forming it. Don't worry! The outside will crisp up, and the inside will be juicy when the meatloaf is done. As you already know, cold leftover meatloaf makes an unquestionably fabulous sandwich. I prefer to cook meatloaf with the tomato sauce served on the side so that the leftovers can be prepared in any number of ways. Try it with whole grain mustard and cornichons.

3 ounces dried wild mushrooms (porcini, chanterelles, etc.) soaked in hot water for at least 20 minutes, drained, rinsed, and coarsely chopped

1 tablespoon extra-virgin olive oil

1 cup chopped shallots

½ cup chopped sweet red pepper

1½ teaspoons finely chopped garlic

½ pound small cremini mushrooms, sliced

1 large egg, beaten

½ cup freshly grated Parmigiano

¼ cup chopped basil

2 tablespoons chopped parsley

1 tablespoon Worcestershire sauce

Coarse or kosher salt and freshly ground pepper to taste

1 cup day-old country bread, coarsely crumbed in a food processor (flavored bread such as a rosemary–olive oil loaf works nicely here)

¼ cup heavy cream or milk

1 pound ground beef

1 pound ground turkey

4 ounces *pancetta*, thinly sliced (and unrolled if possible)*

Long-Simmered Summer Tomato Sauce (page 59)

1. Preheat the oven to 375 degrees.

2. Heat a large skillet over medium heat and add the olive oil. Sauté the shallots, sweet red pepper, and garlic until soft, about 4 minutes. Add all of the mushrooms and stir to incorporate. Cook until the mushrooms are fully coated and just begin to wilt. Remove the vegetable mixture to a large bowl and set aside to cool slightly.

* La Quercia of Norwalk, Iowa, makes an excellent flat *pancetta*.

3. Stir the egg, cheese, basil, parsley, Worcestershire sauce, and salt and pepper into the bowl with the cooked vegetables. In a small bowl, stir the cream into the breadcrumbs. Blend the meat with the vegetables and add the breadcrumb mixture.

4. Pack the meat mixture into an oiled loaf pan or baking dish, and form into an oval or rectangle. Drape the loaf with the unrolled *pancetta*, as you would with bacon strips. Otherwise, cut and fit the *pancetta* over the loaf and place the pan in the oven.

5. While the meatloaf is cooking, heat the tomato sauce. Bake the meatloaf for approximately 50 to 60 minutes or until an instant-read thermometer inserted into the center registers 155 degrees. Remove from the oven and let rest for 10 minutes. Slice and serve with the warmed sauce.

Pan-Roasted Veal Chops with Sage

SERVES 4

There may be no meat as delicate as a good veal chop—in the right hands. The shoe that Charlie Chaplin ate in *The Gold Rush* was likely more flavorful than the deadly breaded veal cutlets we had at home. People of descent other than Italian are always surprised when I recount the woeful tales of my mother's cookery. Even more of a surprise for me is when I tell other folks from Italian families, because quite a few of them tell me that they thought they were the only ones whose mothers were terrible cooks. Italian Americans of the same fate, you are not alone!

Veal chops are often grilled, but pan-roasting them with sage and butter gives the bonus of a lovely sauce. Serve this with a simple salad of mixed young greens and fresh tomatoes. Veal pairs well with so many wines, but I would serve this with a Brunello or a Bordeaux.

    4 veal loin chops approximately 1 inch thick
    1 medium clove garlic, peeled and smashed
    Coarse or kosher salt and freshly ground pepper to taste
    2 tablespoons unsalted butter
    1 tablespoon extra-virgin olive oil
    15 to 20 sage leaves, depending on size

1. Rub the veal with the garlic and discard the latter. Season the veal lightly with salt and pepper.

2. Melt the butter and oil in a large skillet over medium heat and add the sage leaves. Add the chops and cook for 3 minutes. Flip the veal and cook for another 3 minutes. Continue cooking until the internal temperature reaches 125 to 130 degrees for medium-rare. Remove and let rest for 5 minutes. Drizzle the chops with pan juices and sautéed sage. Serve immediately.

Veal Cutlets with Truffles alla Bolognese

SERVES 4

One would think that veal would have been a favorite in our household, but it was treated with the same blatant disregard as was lamb and pork. My mother also cloaked them in a diabolic composite called "Italian Breadcrumbs." Whatever their makeup, they tended to aid in the incineration of the veal.

This is a recipe culled from Pellegrino Artusi's *La scienza in cucina*: *Cotolette di Vitella di Latte coi Tartufi alla Bolognese* (Bolognese Style Veal Cutlets with Truffles). First, I must confess that I have only had the slightest of tastes of fine truffles. White button mushrooms were the only edible fungus that graced our table, save for the little jars of Green Giant or B in B (Broiled in Butter) mushrooms. Although I have not found an edible mushroom I would not call a friend, truffles are still well out of my league. Artusi does not specify which truffles to use. I have tried this recipe with jarred black summer truffles, which will not cost you your firstborn. If your truffles do not have a rich enough taste, you can always cheat and sprinkle them with a splash of truffle oil. Artusi recommends veal cut from the lean part of the leg and pounded *della dimensione della palma di una mano*—basically, to the size and shape of the palm of your hand. Since this recipe was published in 1891, and Artusi had little care for exact amounts, the ingredients he lists are not precise. I have offered what feel to be the appropriate amounts. If you are a fan of veal *parmigiana*, try this pleasing and unusual variation.

8 sliced and thinly pounded veal cutlets

FOR THE MARINADE:

½ cup freshly squeezed lemon juice

Coarse or kosher salt and pepper to taste

¼ cup Parmigiano

1 egg at room temperature, lightly beaten

FOR THE MEAT:

2 tablespoons butter, or more as needed

Breadcrumbs to coat

As many summer truffles as you can muster, thinly sliced

8 thin slices Gruyère

½ cup beef broth

Freshly squeezed juice from 1 small lemon

1. Place the cutlets in a wide, shallow bowl and marinate with the ½ cup lemon juice, salt and pepper, and Parmigiano. Let stand for 1 to 2 hours. Add the egg and let stand for another 1 to 2 hours.

2. Melt the butter in a large frying pan over medium-high heat. Shake off excess marinade and dredge in breadcrumbs. Add the cutlets to the pan when the froth of the butter has subsided. You will probably need to do this in batches if necessary, adding more butter as needed. When browned on one side, flip the cutlets and brown on the other side. This may take about 2 minutes for each side.

3. Return all the veal to the pan. Cover the veal with truffle slices and top with the Gruyère. Add the broth and simmer for about another 2 minutes or until the cheese begins to melt. Remove the cutlets to a warm platter, pouring the pan juices around them, and topping them with the lemon juice.

Ossobuco Milanese

SERVES 4

We had a dog—Chips. He was the repository for bones. Otherwise, apart from spare ribs, all the food that appeared on our plates was miraculously shorn of any sign of internal structure. Roasts, chops, and even chicken were all boneless. The idea of serving a meal that was primarily bone—and with the marrow—would have Chips intermittently snarling and laughing at us.

So where would we be without *ossobuco*? Well, without *ossobuco*, for one—and that would be a tragedy befitting Shakespeare at his most glum. There are two types of *ossobuco*, or, roughly, "bone in the hole": a modern version that has tomatoes; and the original version, which does not. The older version, *ossobuco in bianco*, is flavored with cinnamon, bay leaf, and *gremolata* (a blend of grated orange and lemon peel, parsley, and garlic). The modern and more popular recipe includes tomatoes, carrots, celery, and onions. One finds that the *Gremolata* is also optional in many recipes today. *Risotto alla Milanese* is the traditional accompaniment to *ossobuco in bianco*, served together making for a one-dish meal. *Ossobuco* can also be served with polenta or mashed potatoes. Outside Milan it is sometimes even served with broad pasta noodles.

Although the use of marrow bones and veal shanks was common in Italian cuisine during the Middle Ages, Milan claims to be the birth city of *ossobuco*. To prove their point, in 2007, the city council declared that *ossobuco* was part of the *De.Co.* (*Denominazioni Comunali*, or community denominations), which is an official public acknowledgment that a dish belongs to that region and that region alone. The recipe is believed to have first appeared in Pellegrino Artusi's cookbook. It seems he would concur with the later edict, as he maintains, "This is a dish that should be left to the Milanese to make for it is a specialty of Lombardy cuisine. Therefore, to avoid ridicule, I shall describe it briefly." At the expense of ridicule, I present it here.

½ cup flour
Salt and freshly ground pepper, to taste
4 pieces veal shank with bone, cut 3 inches thick
4 tablespoons butter
1 cup chopped onion
½ cup chopped celery
½ cup chopped carrots
2 tablespoons coarsely chopped garlic
2 bay leaves
2 tablespoons finely chopped parsley
1 cup dry white wine
2 cups veal or chicken stock
2 cups peeled, seeded, and chopped tomatoes
1 teaspoon grated lemon peel
1 teaspoon grated orange peel

1. Combine the flour and salt and pepper on a large, shallow platter. Dredge the veal shanks in the mixture and tap off any excess. Heat the butter in a large, heavy skillet or Dutch oven over medium heat until foamy. Add the shanks and brown on all sides.

2. When the shanks are nicely browned, add the onion, celery, carrots, 1 tablespoon of the garlic, the bay leaves, and parsley to the pan and cook until softened, about 2 minutes.

3. Add the wine and cook and deglaze the pan until completely reduced. Then pour in the stock and set to a simmer. Set the shanks upright so as to keep the marrow from leaking out, and add the tomatoes to the pot. Bring to a boil. Reduce the heat to low, cover, and cook for about an hour or until the meat is tender. Baste the meat a few times during cooking.

4. Remove the cover, raise the heat slightly, and continue to simmer for 10 minutes to reduce the sauce a bit. Stir in the grated lemon peel and grated orange peel and the remaining 1 tablespoon garlic, and cook for another minute or two. Remove the bay leaves and season with salt and pepper to taste.

Baked Lamb with Fingerlings and Grape Tomatoes

In the course of my in-laws' business, they had employed the talents of a marble worker and his family in the hills of Carrara. Valdina was working for her parents at the time, and we had the pleasure of meeting the marble worker's family and dining with them in their two-hundred-year-old home. The father had probably the largest hands I'd ever seen on a human. Being as dexterous as he was with cutting and shaping marble, he was hardly ham-fisted, but his palms alone were as big as any Smithfield.

As was the custom with many rural Italian families, their son and daughter-in-law also lived and worked with them. Entirely the antithesis of the lifestyle I grew up with, they lived off the land and prepared most of their meals from the food they grew and the animals they raised. Their dedication to this humble way of life was so steadfast that the mother of the household was greatly embarrassed by her daughter-in-law's decision to purchase a cake in town for our dessert. I don't remember the cake, but I cannot forget the lamb that they had slaughtered earlier that day and served for dinner. I did my darnedest to get the recipe from the mother. Like most Italians she was entirely forthcoming, but *"un po' di questo, un po' di quella"* (a little of this, a little of that) did not in the least smack of specificity. This is my approximation of her incredible stew. Once again, although there is white wine in the dish, red wine should go into the glass. Apart from the usual suspects, you may also serve a Sangiovese or a Cabernet Sauvignon.

3 tablespoons extra-virgin olive oil, and more as needed

2 tablespoons butter

3½ pounds leg or loin, cut into 2-inch pieces and patted dry

1 cup chopped onion

Coarse or kosher salt to taste

1 cup dry white wine

2 tablespoons finely chopped fresh rosemary

1½ teaspoons finely chopped garlic

¾ pound grape (or cherry) tomatoes, halved and seeded

1 pound small fingerling or new potatoes, scrubbed lightly but
not peeled

Freshly ground pepper to taste

1. Heat a large, heavy-bottomed casserole or Dutch oven with lid over medium-high heat. Add the olive oil and butter and heat until they are very hot and the foam of the butter has subsided. Working in batches, brown the meat on all sides, 8 to 10 minutes per batch. Remove the last batch and fry the onion in the pot until soft, about 4 minutes. Add more oil if necessary. Meanwhile, heat your oven to 350 degrees.

2. Pour the wine into the pan and, using a wooden spoon, scrape the browned bits stuck to the bottom of the pot. Return the meat to the pan with the onions, and sprinkle with salt. Add the rosemary and garlic and cook another minute. Stir in the tomatoes and cook uncovered for 15 minutes.

3. Add the potatoes to the meat. Cover the pot and place it on the center rack of the oven. Stir from time to time, and cook until the meat is very tender, 2 to 2 ½ hours. Add freshly ground black pepper and more salt to taste. Serve with crusty country-style bread and a simple salad.

Grilled Pork Chops (Braciole di Maiale)

SERVES 6

In Italian American cuisine, *braciole* (often pronounced *bra'zhul* from the Sicilian dialect) is the name given to thin slices of meat (typically pork, chicken, or beef, but even swordfish) that are rolled as a *roulade* with cheese, with or without breadcrumbs, and fried. This was not how I understood the word when I was growing up. The Italian "gentlemen" of the neighborhood would casually refer to any comely woman as such. Naturally when I heard an adult use the term *braciole* in a restaurant, my eyebrows took to the sky. If you have watched several episodes of *The Sopranos*, you have heard that the word has retained its dual meaning. When I was researching my family's southern Italian roots, I came upon this embarrassingly simple recipe from Calabria. As you will see, it bears no resemblance to either Italian American derivations. These are thin chops and will cook quickly, so be vigilant. The simplicity of this dish also calls for a simple wine, such as a young Pinot Noir or a Merlot.

> 6 boneless pork loin chops about ½-inch thick
> 1 teaspoon finely ground crushed red pepper
> 2 teaspoons freshly ground fennel seeds
> Coarse or kosher salt and freshly ground pepper to taste

1. Gently pound the chops with a frying pan or the side of a cleaver to flatten them to ¼ inch. Rub them with finely ground crushed red pepper, fennel seeds, and salt and pepper to taste. Let them rest at room temperature for 15 minutes.

2. Light a hardwood charcoal fire, or preheat a gas grill, and lightly oil the grate when the fire reaches medium-high. Grill the chops for 2 to 3 minutes per side until the internal temperature reaches 135 degrees for medium. Serve immediately.

Roasted Rosemary Chicken and Potatoes with Balsamic Vinegar

SERVES 4 TO 6

I met Lynne Rossetto Kasper nearly two decades ago, right after her now near-legendary *The Splendid Table* was published. Her book is in the small pantheon of great Italian cookbooks—wherever that is. At the risk of sounding sycophantic, if there are two Italian cookbooks you should own, you'll want this one (I'll let you pick the other). Even though I am a dyed-in-the-blue-pinstripes Yankees fan, it was more gratifying for me to meet her than it was to meet Mariano Rivera—and Derek Jeter. I by no means intend to imply that I have in any way improved on her sumptuous recipe for roasted chicken, but as a garlic lover (even more than a Yankees fan) I offer a plebeian twist. The original idea was to rub garlic and rosemary into a chicken from the outside before roasting. I have opted to blend the mixture with butter and place it under the skin. This is the perfect occasion to use the precious drops of your finest balsamic vinegar.

2 tablespoons minced fresh rosemary
1 tablespoon minced fresh flat-leaf parsley

1 tablespoon minced fresh chives

2 tablespoons minced garlic

Coarse or kosher salt and freshly ground pepper

4 tablespoons unsalted butter, softened to room temperature

4- to 5-pound organic free-range roasting chicken

1 small lemon, quartered

6 sprigs rosemary

¾ pound mixed small Yukon gold and new potatoes, scrubbed and halved

¼ cup dry white wine

3 to 4 tablespoons Tradizionale di Modena balsamic vinegar

1. Preheat the oven to 400 degrees.

2. In a small bowl, combine the herbs, garlic, and half the salt and pepper you intend to use, and the butter. Blend together until all of the ingredients are fully incorporated.

3. Rinse the chicken under cold running water and dry it thoroughly. Place it breast-side up on a platter and carefully push your fingers under the skin to separate the skin from each side of the breast, creating two pockets. Setting aside 1 tablespoon of the herb mixture, divide the rest into two portions and spread each portion evenly into one of the pockets. Rub the outside of chicken with the remaining tablespoon of herbed butter and sprinkle with the rest of the salt and pepper. Put the lemon quarters and two rosemary sprigs in the bird's cavity. Keep the remaining rosemary sprigs for garnishing.

4. Set the chicken on its side on a rack in a small baking dish or roasting pan and spread the potatoes evenly around it. Pour in the wine. Roast for 20 minutes and then turn the bird on its other side and cook for another 20 minutes. Baste the bird and the potatoes every 10 or 15 minutes as soon as juices accumulate in the pan. Flip the bird on its back and roast for another 20 minutes per pound. Lower the heat to 375 degrees and roast for 15 minutes or until a thermometer tucked into the thickest part of the thigh or leg reads 165 degrees (1¼ to 1½ hours) and the juices run clear.

5. Transfer the chicken from the baking dish to a platter, loosely cover with foil, and let it rest for 10 minutes. Carve into 8 serving pieces (legs, wings, and breasts split and halved). Garnish with the remaining rosemary sprigs and drizzle each piece of chicken with the vinegar.

Fricassee of Chicken

SERVES 4

What's in a name? When it comes to "fricassee," it's too much or not enough. For many people it's a bland white stew, with bland white chicken and bland white dumplings. Meanwhile, Julia Child in *Mastering the Art of French Cooking* describes it as "halfway between a sauté and a stew" in that a sauté has no liquid added, while a stew includes liquid from the beginning. In a fricassee, cut-up meat is first sautéed (but not browned), then liquid is added and the meat is simmered to finish cooking. In 1490, the dish is first referred to specifically as "*friquassee*" in the print edition of *Le Viandier*. As you can imagine, any dish that has been around for more than half a millennium will have undergone a few changes. Chicken fricassee was one of Abraham Lincoln's favorite dishes, and if you can also imagine that the following dish had any similarity to what he forked on his plate, you're better than me.

This is a dish that I cook at least once a month, and we never tire of it. If I were to say that I eat more chicken now than I did growing up, it is because I never had chicken growing up, except perhaps in Chinese takeout. It was probably too much work. When I did finally come around to cooking chicken, it was usually boneless chicken breasts. As with turkey, I only ate the white meat at first. I have since come to prefer the rest of the bird, particularly the thighs.

Many cooks use the entire chicken for their fricassee, but I think you get more cluck for your buck by just cooking the thighs.

2 tablespoons olive or canola oil
4 large bone-in chicken thighs, skin on, about 2 pounds or so
Coarse or kosher salt and freshly ground black pepper
2 tablespoons chopped garlic
1 tablespoon chopped fresh rosemary
½ teaspoon crushed red pepper, or more to taste
¾ cup dry white wine
About 20 or so small grape tomatoes
About 20 or so small Kalamata or other European black olives

1. Heat the oil in a large skillet over high heat. Rinse the chicken, pat it dry, and add it, skin-side down, to the hot oil. Do not turn until one side is completely brown.

2. Turn the chicken to the other side and sprinkle with salt, pepper, garlic, rosemary, and crushed red pepper. When the second side is completely browned, add the white wine, scraping the brown bits in the bottom of the pan.

3. As soon as the wine comes to a boil, turn the heat down to low and cover. Cook slowly for an hour or more, turning the chicken every 15 minutes, until the chicken is tender and nearly coming off the bone.

4. Add the tomatoes and olives, and cook uncovered until the skin on the tomatoes begins to wrinkle. Add a few splashes of water if the liquid has reduced too much. Serve immediately with rice or roasted potatoes.

Pizza

You've tried all the rest, now try the best!

Or so says the inscription on many a take-out pizza box. "Pizza," from the Italian word *pizzetta*, meaning "piece," may be the single most identifiable food in the world. The Swiss invented kebab pizza; there is "Abalone Sauce Cheesy Lava Stuffed Crust Pizza" in Hong Kong; "Banana Curry Pizza" in Sweden"; "Whole Shrimp Cheese Bite Pizza" in Japan, with a ring of shrimp with tails dangling in the air and heads swaddled in tubes of cheese-stuffed dough; and an Australian Pizza Hut offered free pets to customers making bulk purchases (which I trust was not a do-it-yourself topping).

Creativity and lunacy aside, the most common of all pizza toppings are tomato and cheese. In the book *La Neapolitan Pizza*, Gabriele Benincasa claims that the earliest pizzeria, owned by Giovanni Calicchio, was already in business by 1760. However, it was in the Pizzeria Brandi, which is still in business today, that Raffaele Esposito woke up all of Naples to the joy of cooking, and eating, pizza with the *pizza alla Margherita*. Originally created as a special dish for Italy's queen consort Margherita when she made a visit to Naples in 1889, this pizza was made with three ingredients as a reference to Italy's red, white, and green flag: tomato, mozzarella, and basil. Here's yet another bit of trivia: the last name *Esposito* came from *"senza esse sposata"* meaning "without being married." When the women of Naples gave birth to a child and no formal husband was listed in the registry, that child's last name would be Esposito.

Prior to the World War II, this dish was little known in Italy outside of Naples. But due to the influx of Neapolitan immigrants to the East Coast of the United States, pizza was already a well-established dish in cities like New York, New Haven, Boston, and Philadelphia. The first recorded venue where pizza was sold in the States was the grocery store G. Lombardi's on Spring Street in New York. According to John Mariani in *The Dictionary of Italian Food and Drink*, pizza was more familiar to the Italians in New York or Baltimore than it was in Italy. By 1950, pizza began to catch on in Italy. Today there are pizzerias throughout the land of its birth, with about 5,000 ovens in Naples alone, all serving up a total of about 2.5 billion pizzas a year—all thanks to our Neapolitan immigrants. Meanwhile, the number of pizza parlors in the United States skyrocketed from 500 in 1934 to 20,000 in 1956. Today there are more than 70,000 in the $37 billion U.S. pizza industry.

For notable Italians living in this country, pizza was still peasant food. In 1959 Sophia Loren told the Los Angeles Times that, having been raised in Italy, she considered pizza the food of poverty. She initially pitied Americans when she saw how many pizza parlors there were here. "So I think America not so rich after all. Then I find eating pizza here is like eating hot dog—for fun." She clearly changed her tune completely by 1971 when she published her memoir/cookbook *In cucina con amore*, in which she is shown happily making and flipping pizza dough.

I am given to exaggeration, but rarely hyperbole. That I can say that I am passionate about pizza is no exaggeration. One might wonder how that arose in a house where the only pizza we made at home came frozen from a box, or else it was a slapdash toaster-oven-baked English muffin slathered with jarred sauce and topped with mozzarella cheese. Outside the house it was difficult to get mediocre pizza in New York right into the 1970s. You could also find it in the most unlikely places. Many taverns and bars in New York made fine pizza. This makes perfect sense, since the cooks in the back kitchen still tended to be Italian. Alas, however, we did not have a pizzeria or tavern nearby. Takeout was usually so far away that the pizza, though still good, was not the same when it arrived home. Neither my father nor my mother drove; so I would either trek down to Jamaica with friends to buy a couple of slices and a soda at Tony's (for the price of forty cents total), or it was a special outing to a restaurant.

I was such a fiend for pizza that I would do my darnedest to savor as much as I could in the restaurant, but I also made sure that I had more to munch on while driving home. Since none of my parents' friends would tolerate a kid messing up the upholstery of their cars by eating a precarious slice of pizza, I devised a perfect solution. I would eat all of the pizza up to the crust in the restaurant, and then save the crust in a napkin, and eat it later (the crust, that is). It was *amore*! Speaking of which, Dean Martin thought the lyrics "When the moon hits your eye like a bigga pizza pie / That's amore!" were ridiculous. He almost did not record the song, but after being featured in *The Caddy* (1953), "That's Amore!" hit number two on the Billboard charts, no doubt making Dino quite pleased that he had been persuaded otherwise.

When I ventured outside the immediate New York area, there wasn't any decent pizza to be found. It was like being in a wasteland. (What did I know of places like New Haven?) Addict though I was, I would settle for anything remotely resembling it. During our annual two-week stay in a godforsaken place called Honesdale, Pennsylvania, not only was there but one, rather hazy, TV channel, but there were no restaurants. One day, choosing not to stay home watching the weeds grow or taunting my sister, I accompanied my mother and my aunt to a small department store in Carbondale. It should have been painfully obvious that the town was named for the element carbon: coal. But how was I to know that Carbondale was the site of the first deep vein anthracite coal mine in the United States, and that by 1946 it had been so riddled with holes like a piece of lacy Swiss cheese that almost fifty acres of mine collapsed simultaneously, killing hundreds?

This might have come as an astonishing tale, but to my more immediate amazement, there was a lunch counter at the town's wannabe Woolworth's that offered pizza! The guy behind the counter was a bit miffed because he said he had to make it from scratch, and it would take a while. Little did he know that I would rather watch pizza being made than try to tune in a rerun of *Superman* on the single-channel TV. Leaning slightly over my Classics comic book of ghost stories, I studied him as he pulled a plastic bag from beneath the counter and extracted a white disk that was undoubtedly the dough. He commenced making his pizza "from scratch" by opening a bag of red and pouring it over the white disk. Then he opened yet another small bag of white, which was apparently cheese. After about 10 minutes more of salivating on my part, voilà! Pizza! Well, sort of, but it worked for me.

Despite anything you may have heard, there is no shortcut to making truly remarkable pizza. Yes, there are recipes for decent pizza that can be prepared in one day, but for a better pie, the dough should remain in the refrigerator at least overnight. For an even better pizza still, the dough should go through several slow rises, with two trips to the fridge. For pizza the same night, I would recommend the recipes in Peter Reinhart's *American Pie*, or you may Google Jeffrey Steingarten's recipe. These are both excellent sources, but after thirty-five years of personal experimentation, the following recipe is the one I have found to be the best. I offer no alternatives, because there are other limitless recipes out there to choose from.

The first step is the flour. At this point in my pizza making I only use Caputo 00 flour, imported from Italy. What was once a grail for home pizza makers can now be readily found on the Web or in specialty markets. King Arthur makes an excellent line of flours, but I have found that the Caputo provides just the right crunch and rise in the baked dough. The rest of the ingredients are just yeast, water, and salt.

When eating out, though, I would never confine myself to this type of pizza. In fact, some of the best pizza I have had in this country has olive oil incorporated in the dough: Neo-Neapolitan pizza. Most New York joints and the mecca of New England pizza pilgrims, Pepe's on Wooster Street in New Haven, all use olive oil. The food writer Michael Stern was asked if he were to choose a last meal, what it would be. Without hesitation, he said a Pepe's white clam pie. And so if I want a stellar pie made with olive oil, I dash down to Pepe's. A hundred or so miles is hardly a dash for us, but the anticipation makes it seem like one. At home, however, I follow the traditional Italian method of forgoing the oil, except to lightly coat the bottom of the dough's rising surface.

As for fresh mozzarella in the States, it has come a long way, but it has not quite arrived. Apparently it's all in the milk. As I have mentioned earlier, the best mozzarella is made from milk that comes from a particular breed of water buffalo in Italy. Some ardent American cheesemakers spend their waking hours attempting to reproduce the silky, milky smooth mozzarella spun in Italy, and one tenacious cheesemaker has even taken to raising a similar breed of water buffalo in his quest for the genuine article. To my amazement, however, I have had a splendid buffalo mozzarella from—of all places—Colombia. It is a handcrafted, organic cheese from free-range grass-fed water buffaloes, and it rivals some of the Italian brands I have tasted.

Pizza Dough

If you were to follow the Italian approved method for "Verace Pizza Napoletana" (*Vera Pizza Napoletana*), the Associazione Verace Pizza Napoletana has provided an eleven-page list of rules and regulations you must adhere to in order to produce a true Neapolitan pizza. To comply, in addition to using water with an exact pH (6–7), following specific times and stages for raising the flour, and setting your oven to the precise temperature (485 degrees C/905 degrees F), the finished pie should be consumed only immediately after coming out of the oven— *the pie can only be eaten at the pizzeria.* So much for cold *Vera Pizza Napoletana* for breakfast.

An important note: Most recipes do not tell you this, but salt can kill yeast. Do not add it until the dough has begun to come together.

Since this is a rather rigorous method you won't be trying very soon, I offer a humble alternative.

> **An important note:** *Most recipes do not tell you this, but salt can kill yeast. Do not add it until the dough has begun to come together. I cannot imagine how many people have wondered why their dough did not pan out as expected. The reason was that the recipe they read said to add the salt at the beginning.*

1 teaspoon SAF Instant Yeast Red Label
2 cups warm water, or more if needed
6 cups 00 flour, plus more for dusting
1 tablespoon coarse or kosher salt
Olive oil

1. In a stand mixer fitted with a dough hook, whisk the yeast with ¼ cup of the water and let stand until it is just becoming foamy, about 5 minutes.

2. Add the flour to the yeast mixture, and slowly pour in the rest of the water. Turn the mixer to the lowest setting and, scraping the sides of the bowl, mix until all of the flour is incorporated, about 5 minutes. Add the salt and mix another minute. Let the dough rest for 5 minutes, and then continue mixing until a soft, smooth, slightly tacky dough forms, about 5 minutes longer. Add flour or water as necessary.

3. Scrape the dough out onto a lightly floured work surface (a plastic silicone baking sheet is perfect for this). Lightly flour your hands, and spread the dough into an oblong *ciabatta*, slipper shape, on the floured surface and then fold half of it back over itself. Let the dough rest for another 10 minutes. Form it into a large ball. Transfer the dough to a large bowl dusted with flour, and cover tightly with plastic wrap. Place the dough in a warm, dark place and let it rise until it has doubled, from 6 to 8 hours. Refrigerate the dough overnight.

4. Remove the dough from the fridge and allow it to return to room temperature, about 2 hours.

5. Scrape the dough out onto a lightly floured work surface and cut the dough and form 3 equal balls. If you are fortunate to have those aluminum pizza proofing pans, great! Otherwise, lightly oil a large baking pan with sides. Place the dough balls a distance apart in the pan and lightly dust with flour. Tightly cover the pan with plastic wrap, avoiding the wrap touching the dough. As with the first rising, place the dough in a warm, dark place and let it rise until it has doubled, from 6 to 8 hours. Refrigerate the dough overnight.

6. About 2 hours before you want to prepare a pizza, remove the dough from the fridge.

My Basic Pizza Sauce

You will find most recipes calling for a cooked sauce. I disagree. If you have fresh or good canned tomatoes, they will cook in the oven on the pizza. If the sauce is cooked ahead of time, there is a chance it may become bitter in the second cooking in the oven.

> 2 small cloves of garlic, lightly crushed
> 1 28-ounce can whole San Marzano or Muir Glen tomatoes
> 1 tablespoon extra-virgin olive oil
> Coarse or kosher salt to taste

With your food processor going, add the garlic through the feed tube. Stop and open the food processor to scrape the garlic down and then add the olive oil. Pulse quickly. Scrape the bowl down again and add the tomatoes. Pulse until smooth, but not watery. Transfer to a bowl until ready to use.

Basic Pizza Margherita

Flour for your work surface (this can be regular unbleached
white flour)

½ cup pizza sauce of choice

¼ pound fresh mozzarella cheese, thinly sliced (or small rounds
of buffalo milk mozzarella if available)

16 fresh basil leaves

Extra-virgin olive oil, for drizzling

2 tablespoons freshly grated Parmigiano-Reggiano

1. Let your pizza dough rise again at room temperature for about 2
hours. If you have two pizza stones, all the better. Place one stone on
the bottom rack of the oven and the other on the second to the top.
If you have one stone, place it in the lower third of the oven and turn
your oven to its highest setting for about an hour for optimum heat.
If you have a convection feature, turn that on as well.

2. Lightly dust a pizza peel or suitable wide flat baking sheet with flour
(not cornmeal). Working on a heavily floured surface, press and stretch
a dough ball from the center outward into a thin round, leaving the
edge slightly raised. Turn several times to make sure that the dough
is well-floured and not sticky. Carefully slide the dough onto the peel.

3. Working quickly, add the sauce, spreading it evenly, but leaving a
1-inch border around the edge. Top with the mozzarella and the Parmigiano. Lightly drizzle with olive oil and sprinkle on half the basil. Slide
the pizza onto the pizza stone. Bake until the bottom is lightly charred
and the toppings are bubbling, about 8 to 10 minutes, depending on the
heat of your oven. Remove the pizza from the oven and sprinkle with
the remaining basil.

For other pizza:

Here are just a few suggested toppings, some unusual ones that you might find only on pizza in Italy, but no doubt you have your own favorites. The key to remember is that you should never overload your dough with too many toppings. Prepare your toppings and set them in an orderly fashion next to your bowl of sauce. You really want to have everything ready at hand so the sauce will not soak in and inundate the dough. Bake as directed above.

COMBINATIONS WITH TOMATOES OR TOMATO SAUCE
Tomato sauce, mozzarella, Parmigiano, onions, and pepper
Tomato sauce, smoked mozzarella, oregano, black olives, and capers
Tomato sauce, fresh mozzarella, anchovies, and oregano
Gruyère, cherry tomatoes, and fresh rosemary
Chopped fresh ripe tomatoes, *lardo*, canned tuna, black olives, and capers
Sliced tomatoes, provolone, porcini mushrooms, and olive oil
Pepperoni or sausage anyone?

WITHOUT TOMATOES OR TOMATO SAUCE
Fontina, Parmigiano, and prosciutto, with arugula added after baking
Provolone, sausage, *lardo*, Parmigiano, olive oil, and basil
Fresh clams, drained, with garlic, Parmigiano, and oregano
Ricotta, egg, Parmigiano, and prosciutto
Potato, provolone, egg, and prosciutto
Pineapple and ham—*DEFINITELY NOT!*

Libations

*The problem with the world is that
everyone is a few drinks behind.*

—HUMPHREY BOGART

The Aperitivo and the Disgestivo

We saw very little alcohol in our home. My father occasionally had a beer or a very light scotch and water. On the other hand, or in the other hand, mother was an absolute teetotaler. At certain holidays she would ask for a Cherry Heering, which was a ghastly cherry liqueur that the kids loved— but I never saw my mother take a drop. An apple falling very far from the tree at times, I took an entirely different direction. Sadly, working in a fine dining restaurant taught me about wine. I say sadly because I can hardly afford what I would like to drink (but we all know that dilemma). Wine and cocktails have become a part of the pleasure of dining, and I add this section to share just a couple of drinks that are essential to the Italian palate.

There are weighty tomes that say nothing, and discriminating brief accounts that speak volumes. Such is the wit and depth of Bernard DeVoto's eloquent paean to cocktail time, *The Hour.* He mused over that peaceful time when the evening cocktail is "the healer, the weaver of forgiveness and reconciliation, the justifier of us to ourselves and one another. One more [cocktail], and then with a spirit made whole again in a cleansed world, to dinner." DeVoto makes the sanctity of the cocktail hour a seemingly epic experience. To this sentiment, the Italian sipping his glass of *spumante* might reply, *"Che cosa?"* "Huh?" Italians have had little regard for hard liquor, although that is gradually changing as the wave of "mixology" is beginning to sweep across Europe.

The emergence of wine dinners has given us the idea that an Italian family may sit down to a four-course meal and pour four different wines. As desirable as this may be, it is not economically—temperately—sound. Families may choose one bottle of wine that will go well with the entire meal. What may be particularly surprising to us is that Italians are drinking less and less wine. This is going hand in hand with the increasing popularity of other, more casual alcoholic drinks—above all, beer, as well as cocktails.

As you might expect, wine and beer are still by far the preferred alcoholic beverages of Italians. Relegating these drinks to a form of sustenance rather than a way to get snookered, they see nothing wrong with watering down wine and giving some to their children. Otherwise, the aperitivo, which is generally low in alcohol by volume (ABV), is a beverage of choice. In Italy it is generally a light alcoholic or nonalcoholic pre-dinner drink served with snacks. *Aperitivo* is derived from the Latin *aperire*, meaning "to open." In this regard, it is an opening of the palate and a tickling of the appetite. It gives friends or relatives a chance to socialize, unwind, and nibble a bit as dinner approaches—or is abandoned entirely if the buffet is formidable. If you are dining out, depending on the bar, you may be served a small tray of anything from a few olives, nuts, and potato chips to fried vegetables, pizza, pasta, and elaborate cold cut platters. Some classic starters are Aperol, Campari, Prosecco, Cynar, a wine spritzer, or a simple glass of vermouth with a dash of bitters and a twist of lemon peel.

After a meal that tends to be heavier, one drinks spirits to aid with digestion. The *digestivo* is often *amaro*, or "bitter." Fernet-Branca and Averna are good examples. Other digestives vary from sweet *limoncello*, to nutty

Frangelico, to the robust *grappa*, the potent libation distilled from the dregs of grapes that have been pressed for wine.

Then there is Strega (or Liquore Strega), an Italian herbal liqueur produced since 1860 in Campania. Its yellow color comes from the presence of saffron in its recipe, and the producers boast of approximately seventy herbal ingredients. Since no one is giving away a trade secret, we'll just have to take their word on that. Nevertheless, mint and fennel are characteristic notes of this *digestivo*. The translation of *strega* is "witch," and, with a whopping 80 proof (40% alcohol) —more than double that of most other *aperitivi* and *digestivi*—you may not need a broom to be flying high after a few of these.

The *digestivo* is almost always served neat and mostly at room temperature, whereas the *aperitivo* is served cold and often mixed with other ingredients. Nonalcoholic *aperitivo* drinks may range from plain soft drinks like Orangina and Coca-Cola to showy fruit-juice cocktails. The three most popular *aperitivi* that Italy has given the world are the Bellini, the Americano, and its more alcoholic kin, the Negroni.

A note on mineral water: All mineral water is clearly, or bubbly, not created the same. If you read the label on the bottle carefully it may say, "sparkling natural mineral water." This means that carbonation has been added to the mineral water. Most mineral water in the United States falls into this category. If the label states, "naturally sparkling mineral water," the water has been carbonated at its source by Nature. The latter are more difficult to find, and they generally have a more mineral taste to them. Apollonaris from Germany is one of the more readily available brands.

I cannot help but include a bit of salty wisdom on imbibing by the outspoken author and critic Jim Harrison from his book of essays *The Raw and the Cooked*: "also, I can't listen to the news without a beverage—the dark tales of how Republican rapacity mated with Democratic desuetude, monitored by a press with moral Alzheimer's has imperiled the republic." I'll drink to that! I better. All the following recipes are for one drink and can be multiplied to suit your company.

Named for the Venetian painter Giovanni Bellini, the Bellini was created at Harry's Bar in Venice in 1948 by the owner Giuseppe Cipriani. This classic refreshing drink was served only in the summer months during the time that white peaches were available. The juice and pulp of the peaches were extracted through a sieve and blended with Prosecco. The rosy-colored elixir became a year-round drink once frozen peach purée was made available. If Venice is not on your travel agenda, you can always visit any of the Harry Cipriani bars in New York during cocktail hour for the perfect Bellini. You will want to stay for dinner, but you may have to sell your firstborn to this end.

Frozen peach purée is difficult to find, so you may be limited to savoring a Bellini during the summer months. Despite what anyone may tell you, only use white peaches for a Bellini—or the color and taste will be off. Another caveat is that you should only purée by hand with a food mill, sieve, or in a metal China cap. For a taste of the Bellini as you might savor it at Harry's Bar, serve appetizers of prosciutto with figs or with mozzarella, and set out a plate of assorted imported olives.

> 1 ounce white peach purée
> 3 ounces Prosecco

You will need to purée the peaches as described above and store the purée in the refrigerator until cold. Following a ratio of 3 parts wine to 1 part purée, serve in a well-chilled highball glass or Champagne flute.

VARIATIONS

Tiziano. Substitute good white grape juice for the peach purée.
Rossini. Substitute strawberry purée for the peach purée.

Americano

The recipe for the Americano dates back to at least 1891, at which time it was served at Gaspare Campari's bar, a meeting place over the years for a variety of celebrities from Giuseppe Verdi to Ernest Hemingway. It wasn't until Prohibition, when Americans were flocking over to Italy for a temporary reprieve, that the drink found favor with the visitors and was dubbed the Americano or American highball. Since the extremely bitter Campari was classified as a medicinal product in the United States, Americans took the recipe home and legally indulged throughout Prohibition. Occasionally referred to as a neutered Negroni, the Americano has found admirers in the oddest places. James Bond, known for his martini intake, was averse to ordering strong drinks in outdoor French cafés. In the novel *From a View to a Kill*, Ian Fleming writes, "No, in cafés you have to drink the least offensive of the musical comedy drinks that go with them, and Bond always had the same thing, an Americano."

Order the Americano at an outdoor café under the stars and imagine you are in Venice—unless you are already in Venice. With just a hint of club soda, the Americano is a short drink that may be served as an *aperitivo* throughout the year. The pronounced tartness of the Americano cries out for the crunch of lighter antipasti such as zucchini crisps, mini pizzas, or batter-fried squash blossoms.

1½ ounces Campari
1½ ounces sweet vermouth
Cold club soda or mineral water

Pour the Campari and vermouth over ice and fill with club soda. Garnish with a thin slice of lemon, lime, or orange.

Negroni

This Italian big brother to the Americano and distant cousin to the martini is so bitter for some that its dissenters swear it should be stored in the medicine chest. Its fanatical adherents bask in its ruddy glow and tongue-tingling taste. Some contend that the classic cocktail dates back to Florence in the 1920s when the flamboyant Count—and noted tippler— Camillo Negroni asked for a splash of gin added to his Americano. Others say that the drink, mixed with vodka or gin, has been around as long as the Americano. The Campari company, itself unsure of the origin, eventually decided that the drink should be called a Negroni to avoid confusion with all the other Campari cocktails. Why is it that some party poopers can't just leave spurious legend alone?

Opt for a Negroni when you want an Americano with a wallop to it. Of course, if you don't want an Americano to begin with, stick with a martini, but next time you are sitting in a *trattoria* or outdoor café feeling adventurous, give it a try. Any culture that gave the world the Renaissance, *Spaghetti alla Carbonara,* and Sophia Loren at least deserves a shot. An antipasti platter, with an array of salty cold cuts, marinated vegetables, and hard cheeses is a crowning touch to the complex body of a Negroni.

> 1 ounce gin
> 1 ounce sweet vermouth
> 1 ounce Campari

Serve in a cold old-fashioned glass over ice and garnish with a slice of orange.

VARIATION

Dry Negroni. Substitute dry vermouth for sweet.
Chantal Martineau of the Food Republic Web site offers this nifty twist. As a variation on the beloved Negroni, swap out the Campari for a 1 to 1 to 1 combo of gin, Aperol, and vermouth. Only, instead of sweet vermouth, use Dolin Blanc, an off-dry vermouth. As she puts it, "it's what a Negroni tastes like through rose-colored glasses."

Some final thoughts

As I mentioned earlier, the very word "restaurant" made me think of Italian food. This was probably because whenever we dined out, it was inevitably at an Italian restaurant. This may be another reason that my mother did not go through the trouble of cooking veal *alla Parmigiana* or shrimp *scampi* at home; someone else could cook it for us—and cook it pretty well. The inevitable result of eating my mother's cooking would be the criticism of how it did not taste like the lasagne in a restaurant. Of course, the food that we ate here in the United States would have been just as foreign to the people of Rome. As John Mariani points out, "New dishes were adapted and elaborated on from old ideas. One will not find terms like veal *Sorrentino*, clams *alla Posillipo*, and fillet of sole *alla Livornese*, on any menu in Italy." Anyone who has watched *Big Night*, and snickered at the woman who wanted an expected side dish of spaghetti with her *risotto*, knows exactly what kind of food Americans came to expect in an Italian restaurant: *Pasta e Fagioli*—"pasta fazool"—with garlic bread; veal *parmigiana* with a side of spaghetti; and mozzarella-laden baked *ziti* or *lasagne*. This Americanization of Italian cooking is so beloved by almost everyone that it has become the most common "ethnic" cuisine served in U.S. households, and even some of the higher-end restaurants are catering to these tastes. Carbone, a *New York Times* three-star restaurant (complete with a tiled floor out of *The Godfather*) prides itself on being a "red-sauce joint." At Carbone you can find old familiars on the menu: *Caesar Salad*, garlic bread, *rigatoni*, and *Lobster Fra Diavolo*—all at prices that would give an Italian grandmother a near-fatal conniption fit.

Gimmicky or not, the difference between Carbone and a local red-sauce joint is that the former uses only the finest olive oils, the best imported pasta from Italy, and the freshest fish to satisfy their clientele. At Carbone (which opened in 2013) there is an exquisite version of veal Parm, but at $50 a plate. It is as large as a Frisbee, topped with ovals of browned buffalo mozzarella and a bright red, summer-fresh, barely cooked tomato sauce. As if that is not enough indulgence, it is served with a fried shaft of veal bone. Garlic bread is extra. At the other end of the spectrum, there is the half-century-plus-old Martio's Pizza Parlour in Nanuet (just minutes from my mom). There you can get all of the "traditional" American Italian fare, from pizza and *manicotti* and baked lasagna and *ziti* to their array of heroes, including the veal Parm, served *with* garlic bread, for $11.95. Although, thanks to the efforts of cooks like Mario Batali and Lidia Bastianich, splendid regional Italian cuisine is beginning to make a strong presence here, the familiar Americanized Italian food still reigns.

But back to the home kitchen. As for cooking, my mother now has an unquestionably legitimate excuse *not to*—she is in her mid-nineties and no longer cooks even for herself. She would adamantly dispute that, however, believing that tossing a frozen "skillet meal" of Bertolli Shrimp Scampi and Linguine in a pan for nine minutes is cooking.

On one of my last visits she asked me to do some shopping for her. At the Super Stop & Shop, with my shopping basket brimming with the jarred sauce, pre-grated cheese, diet soda, nondairy creamer, and the like, I wanted to approach the checkout counter masked. This was the same night that I decided to make dinner for her. I brought some of my Bolognese sauce, Italian *tagliatelle*, and a hunk of Parmigiano-Reggiano cheese. To my dismay, she did not have a substantial pot to cook the pasta. This required me to push the resilient noodles into the boiling water as if I were batting down a nest of wasps. I inquired for a colander—but there was none. And no, there was no cheese grater either. It was as though she was actively trying to deny that home cooking ever existed. It was a good thing I did not need to use the oven, as it had become a receptacle for the overflow of plastic shopping bags from the already full dishwasher. At ninety-five and counting, she still hadn't learned to cook, but, to her defense, she had succeeded in not needing to.

Living into one's mid-nineties, though, proves for some that not only healthful meals will keep you going. Throughout her long life, her food pyramid had been more of a food sepulcher: salt, sugar, processed foods, and preservatives. This is what I grew up with and what she still eats. My sister, Donna, told her one night that she would pick up anything my mother wanted for dinner. She asked for Popeyes Chicken. In this respect, I should paraphrase Duke Ellington regarding our dissimilar tastes: "If it tastes good, it is good." So perhaps my mother was not an assassin after all.

My mother and yours truly, c.1955

Appendices

⁓

APPENDIX 1

The Italian Cookbooks in My Life

Since no Italian recipe has been written in stone, we must realize that no single recipe is sacrosanct, despite the authoritarian conviction that so many writers have about their own recipes. The ingredients may be sacrosanct, but certainly not the way to prepare them. One personal issue I have with the authors of most cookbooks is that they seem to present their recipes as coming entirely from themselves. John Thorne in his brilliant, and highly opinionated *Simple Cooking*, finds it strange that Marcella Hazan never mentions Giuliano Bugialli in all of her work, nor does he mention her. And neither of them whispers the names of Ada Boni or Pellegrino Artusi. I owe a debt to all of them, and, like them, I offer Italian cooking as I have experienced it.

This is my short list of authors and their books that I see as indispensable to Italian cooking: Ada Boni, *Italian Regional Cooking*; Marcella Hazan, *The Classic Italian Cookbook*; Lynne Rossetto Kasper, *The Splendid Table*; Giuliano Bugialli, *The Fine Art of Italian Cooking*; and the Phaidon Press *The Silver Spoon*. One is often hard-pressed to use the word "definitive," but Julia della Croce's beautifully illustrated and informative *Pasta Classica* is about as close as one can get to the primary source for pasta making and cooking. Ada Boni's first American cookbook, *The Talisman Italian Cookbook* (1950), translated from the Italian by Matilde Pei, with an introduction from her father, the aforementioned Mario Pei, was indeed a pioneering work. It was very much the Italian equivalent of *Joy of Cooking*. If Italians owned but one cookbook in English during the late '50s and early '60s, this was it. Judging from reviews on Amazon, it is still revered by a generation of Italians who grew up with it. Unfortunately, the translation of the recipes for this "Special Edition Printed For Ronzoni Macaroni Co., Inc." was adapted for American kitchens of the time. This means that far too many of the recipes substitute ingredients for those that were not available here and are clearly not authentic. For example, all of her *risotto* dishes simply call for rice without any qualification, and the recipes themselves call for the basic method that you would use to cook typical long-grain rice. Of course, there are legions of Italian Americans who have inherited a dog-eared copy from their *nonnas*, and they swear by it. If you can get hold of the 1977 edition of *Il Talismano Della Felicità*, which is four times as long as its American cousin, it is worth learning Italian for. As a final suggestion, albeit not an Italian cookbook per se, I heartily recommend the amiable, iconoclastic John Thorne's *Outlaw Cook* for his refreshingly earthy meditations on cooking as a fundamental process of life.

For the history buffs among you looking for the original recipes for Italian dishes, I would recommend Pellegrino Artusi's 1891 *La scienza in cucina e l'arte di mangiar bene* (*The Science of Cooking and the Art of Eating Well*), published in English with the title *Italianissimo: Italian Cooking at Its Best*. It is truly the first authentic Italian cookbook for the everyday cook, featuring recipes from Italy's many regions. I would also suggest John Mariani's *The Dictionary of Italian Food and Drink*. Like something of an archival truffle hound, Mariani pored over scores of regional Italian cookbooks to recount the origins and authenticity of fifty classic Italian dishes.

Artusi's groundbreaking book is further subtitled *Manuale practico per le famiglie* (A Practical Manual for the Family), and yet he lists almost no amounts for ingredients. This shows how far cookbooks have come from being leisurely travel guides to veritable GPS systems. There were few rules, and therefore few rules to be broken. It would be some time before

Il Duce took over the country, and the equivalent of relentless martinets would begin to take over cookbooks. Also note that Artusi asserts that his book is practical and for the whole family. This manner of thinking is properly known as the "wisdom of the ages." After all, he was a successful businessman by trade. Although few people in cooking circles today have heard of him, that his book came out in ten editions between its initial publication date of 1891 and 1906 says quite a lot about the impact it had on Italian cooking of the time.

Lastly, one of the most unusual and original Italian books on food ever penned is also a "cookbook" that should probably only be read and never cooked from. First published in 1932, *The Futurist Cookbook* by Italian artist and iconoclast Filippo Tommaso Marinetti is a very serious artistic joke, and an attack on traditional cookbooks and cooking. In the words of its English translator Lesley Chamberlain, "*The Futurist Cookbook* had a single function as a cookery book: it explicitly challenged all that was established by Pellegrino Artusi in 1891 *L'arte di Mangiar Bene*, the summit of nineteenth-century family cooking." It was essentially a manifesto, using his "future" foods as a means to attack the sluggish bourgeois past and replace it with the dynamism and technology of the twentieth century. With his *Sculpted Meats*, *Edible Alphabet*, and *Intuitive Antipasto*, he envisioned food scenarios rather than mere recipes, and he anticipated molecular cooking, sculpted food towers, and a low-carb diet by more than half a century. His recipe, or scenario, for *Aerofood* goes as follows:

> The diner is served from the right with a plate containing some
> black olives, fennel hearts and kumquats. From the left he is served with
> a rectangle made of sandpaper, silk and velvet. The foods must be carried
> directly to the mouth with the right hand while the left hand lightly and
> repeatedly strokes the tactile rectangle. In the meantime the waiters spray
> the napes of the diners' necks with a perfume of carnations while from
> the kitchen comes contemporaneously a violent conrumore [music]
> of an aeroplane motor and some dismusica [music] by Bach.

When the mayor of Naples, clearly an advocate of Artusi's book, stated that *vermicelli il pomodoro* was the food of the angels, Marinetti, who contrarily averred that pasta made one heavy and brutish, replied that if this were true, it only confirmed his belief that paradise must be boring. It should come as no surprise that he was one of the first affiliates of the Italian Fascist Party. He probably should have had more spaghetti.

APPENDIX 2

Kitchen Items You Should Not Be Without
and Kitchen Items I Cannot Live Without

A stand mixer, sharp knives, a salad spinner, a pepper mill, a proper corkscrew? These were all items that we somehow managed to do without in our Queens apartment kitchen. Our knife of choice, when we used one, was a Ginsu knife. With TV advertisements hailing it as the *amazing* Ginsu knife, while the announcer barked, "How much would you pay? Don't answer! But wait! There's more!" how could you not "Call now!" given that they had their "Operators standing by"? The first thing I attempted was not effortlessly slicing and dicing a tomato but sawing in half a tin can. Eventually the knife got tucked away in some drawer behind the other knives that could barely cut butter. As it was, Danny Kaye never came to our house to rant about how knives should never be kept in drawers. He was known to have even jumped up on someone's table screaming, "No knives in drawers!" With all of the canned and packaged foods that filled our larder, you hardly needed a sharp knife anyway. If you had an electric can opener and a microwave, you were well on your way in our house.

Without a doubt, the most utilitarian item in our kitchen was the microwave. Despite the early warnings of radiation poisoning and sterility, we were probably the first family on the block to own one. Now you could do without pots and pans when you could nuke a hot dog, zap a potato, or pop popcorn in a jiffy, so to speak—and with no messy cleanup. Like most kitchen equipment that has become a standard in homes and restaurants alike, the microwave has its purpose. Microwaving a roast beef is not one of them.

Otherwise, when it came to gadgets, there were not as many then as there are today, and our household was spared a square egg maker, the "runny nose egg separator," pizza scissors, and Tater Mitts (as seen on TV). Now that such useless trinkets are available, there has been no stopping my mother's side of the family from giving me an electric peeling wand, a salt shooter, and endless cutesy cork pullers. The tubular hand pump with a sharp needle at the end may have been the worst, but there's always next Christmas. (And why is it they never give you any wine?)

Everyone has his or her own preferences when it comes to cooking equipment. The following lists may be redundant, but they may also come in handy when you are deciding to buy gifts in lieu of a peeling wand. Most kitchens have ladles and a variety of large and small metal and wooden spoons, can openers, and so on, but at the risk of being obvious, here is a short list of items that I consider essential for Italian cooking:

- At least one paring knife, an 8-inch chef's knife or 7-inch *Santoku* knife, and a diamond sharpening steel. Remember, you need to keep these sharp. Using your steel more often than not is preferable, as it will save you the trouble and expense of having your knives sharpened professionally.
- A large *and* a small cutting board. I mark mine on each side so I use one side for vegetables and the other for meat.
- A good, sturdy, sharp vegetable peeler—not like the flimsy metal one you may have inherited from your grandmother.

- A Japanese mandoline. Since one is often tempted not to use the guard, or if the guard is lost, I would highly recommend getting cut-resistant gloves. They are also good for protection while shucking oysters.
- A lidded pot that will hold at least a gallon of water for cooking pasta, and a 2-quart saucepan.
- At least a 12-inch skillet (I prefer All-Clad), but 10- and 14-inch are also handy to have. Remember always to heat these skillets before placing food in them.
- A large baking pan for lasagne and other baked dishes.
- A large, sturdy stainless-steel colander.
- Stainless-steel mixing bowls. I never seem to have enough of these, and you can always find sets for next to nothing in thrift shops.
- Small glass prep bowls for your *"mise."*
- Tongs in a variety of sizes. These are endlessly utilitarian and versatile. No proper restaurant is without them.
- Wooden spoons and a pronged pasta paddle.
- A good adjustable pepper mill, with a capacity to vary the grind.
- A large, wide pasta bowl or platter.
- A proper four-sided grater for various cheeses and nutmeg.
- A salad spinner.
- A digital scale.
- An instant-read thermometer and oven thermometer (I prefer one that registers up to 750° rather than the usual 500°).

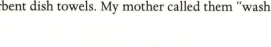

- A fish spatula (really, as I find it more versatile than a flat spatula).
- A two-stage cork puller.
- Plenty of good, absorbent dish towels. My mother called them "wash rags."

- A food processor. I can remember back when, though it is hard to believe, the food processor was scoffed at. Critics have clearly turned around, and it is hard to imagine a restaurant without one. If you can afford it, pay the extra money for a more powerful model with a wide feed tube.

Kitchen Items I Cannot Live Without

In addition to the items listed above, here is just some of the equipment that I constantly rely on:

- A 12-inch chef's knife, a Chinese cleaver, and kitchen scissors (preferably ones that come apart for easier cleaning and sharpening).
- Large and small cutting boards, and a large one exclusively for making pizza and homemade pasta.
- Different vegetable peelers for fine and thicker vegetables and cheese.
- A crescent pasta strainer that fits over the edge of my pasta pot. A fine-mesh strainer and food mill.
- Different size Microplane graters for fine and coarse grating.
- Among other things, a 14-inch sauté pan, a heavy-duty cast-iron pan, a 3-quart saucier pot, and a very large stockpot.
- A stand mixer, and an immersion blender.
- Whisks.
- An electric pasta machine. A manual one is fine, if you have a friend to help you extrude the pasta and prevent it from ending up on the floor.
- A food mill for puréeing tomatoes
- Wide pasta/soup bowls. These should preferably have a wide lip as well to make twirling more, shall we say, delicate.
- A silicone baking sheet. This can also work as a surface for kneading dough.
- A pastry scraper (this is serviceable for cutting dough and smashing garlic as well as scraping vegetables into your bowls).

- 2 heavy, square pizza stones.
- A pizza peel.
- A digital instant-read thermometer.
- A *panini* maker.
- A good cocktail shaker (I don't know about you, but I simply cannot make a weekend dinner without a customary martini.)

I could also create a list of kitchen items I can, and do, live without, but there is probably not enough space in this book. Just go into a Williams-Sonoma, and you will see what I mean. A pasta measuring tool? An avocado slicer? A hedgehog cheese grater? You take it from there.

Mail-Order and Online Sources

These are but a few of the many sites for Italian goods, and beyond. Note that the prices are as varied as the products, but the Web is a perfect venue for comparison shopping. Also bear in mind that the Web sites listed below were entered at the time of writing and some may no longer be up and running. Also always search online to see if there are any coupons available.

- almagourmet.com/store. Alma Gourmet may be my choice for online Italian products because it is a purveyor of almost everything Italian, from cheese and *salumi* to and pastas to housewares. Shipping is ridiculously cheap by comparison with other sources.
- caputosdeli.com. Tony Caputo's Market-Deli is everything an Italian deli should be. The only thing missing from the online shop is the aroma.
- igourmet.com is another of my favorite sites in that it also features a vast array of other international foods.
- eataly.com. Eataly is a trip in itself, but if you cannot make it there, this is their online source for Italian foods and gifts. The prices are high, but at least the shipping is fairly reasonable.
- fairwaymarket.com/marketplace. Fairway is heaven-sent for every manner of ingredient—and at fabulous prices
- ilmercatoitaliano.net. Il Mercato Italiano specializes in imported Italian foods.

- salumeriarosi.com. With locations in Parma, Paris, and New York, Salumeria Rosi offers specialty meats from Italy as well as the United States.
- boccalone.com. Boccalone carries a wide variety of salumi, including *lonza* and *'nduja*.
- laquercia.us. La Quercia in Norwalk, Iowa, produces excellent American versions of cured and specialty meats. Although they do not sell from their Web site, there is a store locator.
- pastacheese.com. Another site for all things Italian is Pasta Cheese Gourmet. They also offer prime meat.
- goitalygourmet.com. Go Italy Gourmet has everything from *sopressata* to Nutella, as well as other international specialties.
- undergroundmeats.com. The Underground Food Collective of Wisconsin in its Underground Meats section specializes in artisanal sausages.
- fgpizza.com. F&G is the place to go for ingredients, and particularly tools that are pizza- and pasta-related for the casual cook and the professional alike. Owners Frankie and Gayle are a pleasure to work with.
- murrayscheese.com. Since 1940 Murray's Cheese has been delighting customers with cheese from around the world. It now has expanded to offer a wide array of specialty meats and other sundries.
- salumicuredmeats.com. Salumi Artisan Cured Meats is the Seattle-based *salumeria* owned by Mario Batali's father, Armandino.
- zingermans.com. Zingerman's features specialty and hard-to-find foods like *guanciale*.
- nolacajun.com/central-grocery-olive-salad. For Central Grocery's olive salad used for making *muffuletta*.
- amazon.com. There is practically nothing that is not available here. Or as one wit said, "Things you can't find anywhere else at prices that can't be beat."

Acknowledgments

It is always a pleasure to collaborate with such a supportive group of people who fully stand behind your work and make every effort to see that it is the best it can be. I want to thank Mary Ann Sabia, Don Weise, and everyone at Charlesbridge for that concerted effort. Having worked as a copy editor as well as a designer, I have often found that the appreciation of these vital fields is often neglected—not here. Maggie Carr did a superlative job editing the text, and the book is now a book thanks to the masterly hand of designer Joe Lops. Lastly, I give my hearty thanks to Ib Bellew at Bunker Hill Studio Books for making this all come together.

Index

Index

641.5945   Chirico, Rob.
CHI

            Not my mother's
            kitchen.

SEP 1 6 2016